STANFORD SERIES IN PHILOSOPHY

Studies in Kant and German Idealism

Eckart Förster, Editor

Aesthetic Judgment and the Moral Image of the World

STUDIES IN KANT

Dieter Henrich

Stanford University Press   Stanford, California

Stanford University Press, Stanford, California
© 1992 by the Board of Trustees of the
Leland Stanford Junior University
Printed in the United States of America

CIP data appear at the end of the book

Original printing 1992
Last figure below indicates year of this printing:
03   02   01   00   99   98   97   96   95   94

Preface

THE JOINT PUBLICATION of these four texts is occasioned by the Kant Lectures delivered in 1990 at Stanford University. I was invited to deliver them in part as a celebration of the two-hundredth anniversary of Kant's *Critique of Judgment*. In the lectures, I discussed two of the most influential theories presented in the first and the very last part of Kant's classic.

The lectures differ in style. The lecture titled "Kant's Explanation of Aesthetic Judgment," which considers the theory in the first part of *Critique of Judgment*, aims to solve a problem to which every student of Kant's aesthetics is exposed, yet which nevertheless proves difficult to state clearly. Its solution depends on how the resources of Kant's epistemology can be employed skillfully within his aesthetics. The lecture shows how this can be accomplished, that Kant himself had only a limited insight into the details of his own theory, and that his fully articulated theory can still contribute to contemporary debates in aesthetics.

The lecture titled "The Moral Image of the World," which considers the theory in the last part of Kant's classic, has a much broader scope. It summarizes the results of my research into the development of Kant's moral philosophy, and it shows that the architecture of the third *Critique* depends upon a change in Kant's notion of a philosophical system, which in turn emerged from an important change in the foundation of his moral philosophy, a change that occurred in the course of his work and reflections on the *Groundwork of the Metaphysics of Morals*.

Kant's conception of a moral image of the world never resulted in a definite explanation of the source and the content of such an image. But Kant, from the days of his encounter with Rousseau's work on, remained convinced of the truth of Rousseau's tenet that, without a moral image of the world, moral conduct itself must become unstable and be undermined by the suspicions of the materialist and the sophist, who are both always already operative in the ordinary man's mind.

I agree with Kant about this. The two texts that constitute the second half of this volume intend to show in what way this view can be put to work within the philosophy of politics. These two texts also originated as lectures, and no attempt has been made to eliminate the traces of their origin.

"The Contexts of Autonomy" was delivered at Emory University, at the conference "Rethinking Human Rights." It has been translated by my former student at Harvard, Professor David Pacini. It first appeared in *Daedalus, Journal of the American Academy of Arts and Sciences*, Fall 1983; the German version has been published as an appendix to my book *Ethik zum nuklearen Frieden* (Ethics Toward Nuclear Peace; Frankfurt a.M., 1990). It appears here courtesy of *Daedalus*.

I gave the lecture "The French Revolution and Classical German Philosophy" at Weimar in May 1989, at a meeting of the Goethe Association, half a year before the collapse of the East German regime and the beginning of the unification of the two German states. The text was published in German in a booklet entitled *Eine Republik Deutschland* (One Republic of Germany; Frankfurt a.M., 1990). It has been translated by Wayne Martin and Sven Bernecker, under the direction of Professor Hans Sluga.

The third lecture argues that the justification of the claim that human rights are universally valid requires reference to a moral image of the world. The fourth lecture conceives of the connection between the political process of the French Revolution and the emergence of post-Kantian philosophy as resulting from the indispensability of a moral image of the world and its justification by fundamentally new political ideas.

To employ the notion of a moral image of the world two hundred years after Kant, yet without ignoring the insights and experiences of this century, requires, to be sure, far-reaching changes in the contents of such an image. The third lecture explains, at least in part, what the content of such an image in our time might consist in.

The four lectures can be jointly regarded as an attempt both to analyze Kant's way of reasoning and to continue it by transforming it to apply to our own questions.

I am grateful to the Philosophy Department of Stanford University for its invitation and its hospitality, to Professor Eckart Förster, who suggested this volume for his series, to Professors Pacini and Sluga and to Mr. Martin and Mr. Bernecker for their translations, and to Helen Tartar and Nancy Atkinson, both of Stanford University Press, who edited my English texts.

Munich   Dieter Henrich

Contents

I

INTERPRETATIONS

ONE

The Moral Image
of the World

THE NOTION OF an "image of the world" has many philosophical implications, one of them clearly Kantian: conceptions of a world arise in particular contexts. It is with regard
to a context that we can account for the constitution a world
exhibits. Such an account requires reference to operations of
the mind, without which the world in question would not be
disclosed to us and could not possibly adopt its shape. In this
way Kant explained nature and the world of nature by means
of rules that guide the synthetic activities we must exert on
what is given to us in sensation.

But the source from which a world originates is equally dependent on that world. Initially it might seem that the principle by which we are capable of accounting for a world
remains independent of what it accounts for. Closer investigation, however, discovers that, unless it executes the activities from which a world originates, the principle itself would
be incomprehensible. This kind of investigation is distinctive
to the method of Kant's epistemology that he calls "transcendental": it can be shown that the unity of self-consciousness
could not even be conceived unless that very unity functions
as the point of departure for constituting a world of objects.

With this, we can understand not only the origin of this world but also why this world is natural and indispensable to us and why our knowledge claims about it are justified.

The same kind of reasoning can be transferred to the field of ethics. Initially, the agent and the moral principles that regulate his conduct again appear to be independent of a particular conception of a world. One could argue that the very notion of a "practical" philosophy precludes any occupation with cosmological and metaphysical problems. Yet this stance conflicts with the fact that the agent and the intelligent person are one and the same subject. And moral actions in particular, as well as their intentions, cannot be regarded as automatic responses to needs or to an environment. In most cases it is possible to avoid these actions. And it is always possible to question why one should act in such a way and thus to doubt the validity of moral claims. But this implies that the moral agent must have thoughts and beliefs about the nature and the sources of his conduct. If that is so, we can also attribute to him beliefs about the world within which he acts and tries to actualize his intentions.

These beliefs are unlikely to correspond in number to the innumerable beliefs we entertain about the world of objects. But they can be equally rich in structure. If the beliefs that are inseparable from the viewpoint of the moral agent are consistent and linked together into a single network, one can call them "a moral image of a world."

But then we might possess two (possibly even more) conflicting conceptions of a world. We certainly cannot claim that the world of objects and the world seen from the moral viewpoint are totally separate. For moral action has as its domain the very situations and circumstances we regard as part of the physical world. Yet physical explanations and the motivation of actions cannot be reconciled, at least not with ease. A relativistic approach, arguing that we need and entertain various images of the world concerning the same worldly affairs, apparently does not suffice, either. It follows that at least the enlightened moral agent needs a moral view meeting two requirements: first, that it relate the various worldviews in some way that prevents their multiplicity from resulting in sheer anarchy or confusion; second, that it survive being exposed to competitors. The moral view must remain reasonable and immune to the charge of arbitrariness and irrationality. Rather, it maintains a certain centrality amidst other views and a certain superiority over them. Once all this has been accomplished, one is entitled to speak of "the moral image of the world" in the singular.

These introductory remarks on the title of this essay may give an idea of the complexity of the problems the very notion of a moral image of the world poses. They also indicate to what extent Kant's philosophy in its entirety can be regarded as a comprehensive solution to just these problems. The three *Critiques* jointly aim at analyzing the constitution of all rational discourses and at investigating the ways in which they originate. Their purpose is to determine the scope and limits of the validity of these discourses and to relate them to one another in a way that can accommodate a legitimate role for the moral point of view and also provide for the design of an adequate and comprehensive moral philosophy whose key concept is the notion of freedom. Therefore, as Kant says in a well-known passage, he had to limit knowledge in order to provide room for belief, a belief that consists in nothing but the content of the moral image of the world. Hence a discussion of the problems arising from the notion of a moral image of the world could very well pave a way into all Kant's philosophy. Here, because I will focus on the *Critique of Judgment*, my approach to these problems will be more historical. This will enable me to locate the *Critique of Judgment* within the development of Kant's thinking about the role of an ethics containing an account of the moral image of the world within the system of philosophy—a system that also aims to understand in depth the conflicts that affect and the forces that motivate a being both rational and human.

The three *Critiques* as a whole will always appear to the uninformed reader to be a monumental monolith with an immensely rich internal structure. One can hardly avoid believing that, before writing the first *Critique*, Kant outlined his program in detail, then carried it out step by step. Such an impression is not entirely misguided, for the fundamental theorems of the first *Critique* remain unchanged and serve continuously as premises in all of Kant's subsequent work. Yet it is equally true that when the first *Critique* was published in 1781, Kant had no definite plans for writing a separate *Critique of Practical Reason*. Instead, the *Groundwork of the Metaphysics of Morals* was intended to provide a foundation for ethics. Moreover, for a while Kant considered including in the second edition of the first *Critique* what would be distinctive to a *Critique of Practical Reason*. He wrote the second *Critique* because his views on the very foundation of ethics changed considerably. As for the *Critique of Judgment*, he arrived at its conception only after he had written the "Critique of Taste"— which he did not conceive before 1786.

These data will already suffice to dissolve the initial impression of Kant's work as a monolith. Kant's thinking remained in constant movement and altered during the period he was publishing it. The same holds true for his later work, up to the point in old age when he began to lose the capacity to control his thoughts and sentences. But even then he wrote about the tantalizing pain of being prevented from completing his work. What he found lacking were not remote applications of his principles, but rather the presentation of the system itself in a new, definitive, and truly comprehensive form.

In a sense, Kant's system certainly has a foundation. It consists in the epistemology of the first *Critique* and the conceptual apparatus operative within it. But it is not a philosophical
foundationalism in any strong sense. The key notion that
leads to the definition of knowledge and provides the justification of our knowledge claims about objects in time and
space is much too weak to suit such a purpose. It provides
only minimal means for relating various discourses to one another. The discourses themselves remain relatively independent. A system can only be envisaged when the way in which
the discourses fit together and complement one another has
been understood. Consequently, the system has to be arrived
at through an ascent—not by means of a logical derivation
from a set of possibly intuitively convincing premises.

It can easily be seen that on the one hand this conception
of the method of systematic philosophy and on the other
hand the conviction that one must assign moral philosophy a
decisive role within the philosophical enterprise correspond
to and support one another very well. Thus one can also expect that a correct understanding of what the moral image of
the world might contain and the localization of such an image
within the network and sequences of discourses would do
more than simply solve a particular problem in an ethics that
maintains that metaphysical views cannot be totally expelled
from ethical questions. The moral image of the world poses a
problem of much wider philosophical interest. Its solution
must contribute to and become an integral component of the
design for a system of philosophy.

That Kant is committed to assessing the status of the problem in this way can already be inferred from the composition
of the *Critique of Judgment*. The book unites its various theories, which might appear to be quite remote from one another, under the notion of a "purpose," thus as theories about
the employment of the notion "purposefulness" in various

contexts. But its introduction is a treatise on the makeup of the critical system at large, and it concludes by assessing the kind of ascent that is distinctively connected with the moral image of the world. The two other *Critiques* conform in their respective ways to the same picture: the second part of the *Critique of Practical Reason* aims to clarify what a "practical usage of reason" might amount to. It too culminates in an exposition of the moral image of the world. As for the first *Critique*, we need only remind ourselves that its argumentation concludes with a chapter on "the ideal of the highest good," which is yet another account of the moral image of the world—a chapter followed only by a final chapter on "the architectonic of pure reason" as such. The moral image and the structure of a system are again closely linked.

This might once again encourage the opinion that Kant had been quite clear all along about the architectural form of his system. One must, however, distinguish his conviction that an understanding of the "moral image" can claim a key role within the system from the stability of his views about the architectonic form of the system as such. Whereas the former remained one of the constants of Kant's thinking from very early on, the latter was gained only after the completion of the first *Critique*. The emergence of a stable view concerning the system's composition has been closely connected with a reorganization of Kant's account of the moral image of the world. We should note in passing that this explains why we find in the first *Critique* statements about the foundations of ethics and the contents of the "moral image" that are irreconcilable with what Kant expounds in the two later *Critiques*. This has confused many of Kant's disciples and interpreters. It has also furnished his contemporary critics with apparently powerful arguments.

These still very general observations may, I hope, arouse curiosity concerning Kant's entanglement with the problems connected with the moral image of the world and the various ways he tried to come to terms with them. We must now turn to the roots of Kant's discussions of the moral image. This will eventually lead us back to the *Critique of Judgment,* but we will then be in a position to assess its doctrines concerning our question as an ultimate yet still transitory state in a long process of reasoning by a great philosopher.

The idea that when it comes under pressure moral conduct needs to be backed up by a conception of the world is as old as our entire philosophical tradition. It is the basic thought in Plato's philosophy. The Sophists had tried to show that one should dispense with the wisdom claimed by the traditional philosophy of nature because it is of no use in practical affairs. They believed that they could do justice to the moral dimension of life by aligning it with everyday experiences and the social traditions of a civilized society. Plato understood the interrogative practice of Socrates, his teacher, as an attempt to show convincingly that the Sophists' move amounted, not to justifying, but to undermining moral insights. Any successful defense of these insights must have recourse to reasons and principles belonging to a totally different dimension—to a theory of the ultimate grounds of all proportions and of all knowledge. It would not, to be sure, revitalize the traditional philosophy of nature. But it would lead to a much more comprehensive theory, whose primary task would be to understand logical and ontological forms as well as to understand the constitution of the mind. Hence one can describe Plato's entire philosophy quite adequately as a device for justifying the moral image of the world. Plato, however, envisaged the philosophical system as a network of insights at which one could arrive by taking the moral life as a point of departure. In itself it is a theory of much broader scope, with its own credentials. It encompasses the moral image, but it does not culminate in it. In this regard, one can view Plato's philosophy as the opposite of Kant's system, though Kant was a Platonist in many other respects.

In Leibniz's philosophy, also, the idea that only a theory of the broadest scope can accommodate the moral dimension looms large. One cannot hope to meet the challenge morality poses to philosophy without conceiving of a "realm of grace" and relating it to the realm of nature in a consistent and perspicuous way.

Kant was well aware of these traditions with which he was connected. He also saw that he would have to reinterpret what he conceived to be the truth within them in a totally new way. There is, however, another philosopher to whom he constantly refers but whom he never quotes when he tries to understand and to justify the moral image of the world. Here Kant finds himself in almost complete accord with him, and one can describe Kant's entire philosophy as the result of an attempt to transform this philosopher's thoughts into a scientifically respectable and universally applicable theory. The philosopher is Jean Jacques Rousseau.

Kant always argued that in philosophizing one must preserve a sober mind. He criticized what he called "enthusiasm" in all of its modes. But he himself could not avoid becoming an enthusiast of Rousseau. He was extremely eager to be informed about Rousseau's fate when he was expelled from Geneva. Rousseau's portrait was the only picture in his study. Moreover, he knew most of Rousseau's work almost by heart. The last can be explained by his report that reading Rousseau inspired him to such a degree that he was unable to examine his thoughts and arguments; his remedy was to read Rousseau's texts continuously over and over until eventually he could calm down. An anecdote reports that only once did he cancel his after-lunch walk (by which his neighbors set their clocks): namely, on the day he received his copy of Rousseau's *Emile*.

The fourth book of *Emile* includes the priest from Savoy's profession of faith. This text is the point of departure for Kant's lifelong attempt to understand and to justify the moral image of the world. Thus we must briefly examine Rousseau's reasoning. The priest's faith is founded on this principle: he will restrict his investigation to those questions that concern him directly and refrain from further philosophical argumentation. Moreover, he will adopt all the propositions that he must approve "in the sincerity of his heart" as the articles of his faith. From this principle arises a reasoning that in part ponders questions of theoretical philosophy, for instance, whether one can understand the existence of the world without tracing it back to an intelligent, active cause (namely, a supreme will) or whether we can understand our own mind and the knowledge it obtains without conceiving of the mind as the source of activities and without attributing freedom to our will. The reasons Rousseau produces were of utmost importance to Kant. For already Rousseau claims that judging is a synthetic activity presupposing a particular unity on the mind's part. Kant pursued these ideas further within his epistemology. The other part of the priest's profession starts with observations on predicaments faced in a morally oriented human life: our conscience requires a certain order of things that is constantly violated by the course of the world. We everywhere observe that wicked persons succeed and flourish whereas the just man remains repressed and persecuted. We cannot accept this state as the last instance or as definitive. Hence we cannot refrain from approving the tenet that there is another life. "If I could have no other proof of the immateriality of the soul than the triumph of evil and the repression of the just in this world, then that would be enough to prevent me from having any doubts about it."

A second, and more important, article of faith originates with another observation: it is conscience that commits me to a way of conduct in the interest of others. Thus it constitutes me as a truly social being. But I cannot justify the demands of my conscience by means of a rational proof. The employment of an unprejudiced reason establishes, rather, that only a well-calculated way of acting in my own interest is rationally justified. But this amounts to a conflict between two descriptions of the world at large. Rousseau calls them explicitly "moral orders." My conscience commits me to belief in the existence of an order whose center cannot be myself. It must have a center about which all agents accord. But my rationality implies the conception of an entirely different order—an order that has as many centers as there are self-interested rational agents.

We don't have any rational proof of the existence of the order of accord. Yet we are utterly unable to accept that our final stance must be belief in the world of rational calculation. Such acceptance would establish what Kant later described as a moral paradox: "If the deity [that is to say, the center of accord] did not exist, only the wicked would reason rationally. The just man would merely be mad." Kant quotes this inference at many places within his moral philosophy without mentioning Rousseau's name. But he could assume that everybody knew to whom he implicitly referred.

A number of comments on Rousseau's reasoning and Kant's way of adopting it are in order.

1. Belief in another life has been based on the disproportionate distribution of luck and happiness within the world we know by experience. Belief in an order that corresponds to the demands of conscience differs from the former belief in that it does not take into account the proportion between moral merit and luck that seems appropriate from the moral viewpoint. It is concerned instead with the *reality* of the moral perspective. If we could not even conceive of another order than the one implied by our rational calculations, we would

have to conclude that the moral perspective is *illusory*. Here the concern is exclusively with the internal coherence of the moral perspective on life and the world that is a prerequisite of its adoption by an agent who is also a rational being. The difference between these two foundational points of reference for the moral image of the world will remain of great importance within Kant's subsequent reflections.

2. Rousseau identifies the center of the order of accord with "the deity." Without hesitation, he understands this to mean the divine person. This is, to be sure, necessary in order to connect belief in the existence of the order of accord to belief in the immortality of the moral agent. The reason for the latter belief was the need to redistribute luck with respect to merit, and it appears that only a divine person is able to assess moral merit. Taken by itself, the order of accord could very well be distinguished from a moral realm having the supreme agent as its governor. Yet once they have been identified, the moral image of the world has been transformed into what Kant calls "moral *theology*." Kant, like Rousseau, had no difficulties in making this step. But Kant, unlike Rousseau, could keep the two moves apart.

3. The reasoning by which the priest from Savoy arrives at the articles of his faith does not address the question in which *way* the content of the moral image is connected with conscience and the viewpoint of the moral life. This connection can be conceived in at least two fashions.

a. Conscience might be self-contained and not at all in need of a conception of the world. Only when it becomes exposed to reflections about its own reality—and hence becomes endangered and torn—need it obtain help from a reasoning that serves its interest. The moral image, thus conceived, is a strategic defense for morality's integrity. The defense might be built up spontaneously, not by detached philosophical speculation. But it would still be a set of beliefs resulting from the needs of conscience, and it would engage other sources than conscience alone, namely, a usage of reason in alliance with the moral interest.

b. One can, however, conceive of the relation between morality and the moral image in a totally different way. The moral image could be a constitutive component of the moral perspective itself. Then one would have to say that conscience and the moral image of the world develop jointly, simultaneously, and as a single, indivisible complex with conscience at its core. It would be pointless to ask for additional resources to provide conscience with an image of the world. The moral agent as such would necessarily possess a perspective not only on his conduct but also on the constitution of the world he belongs to. Hence it would also be pointless to look for reasons that would enable us to build up a moral image. It would be there and operative all along—although a specific moral agent, when questioned by a philosopher, might be unable to articulate her beliefs in words and might not even know that she in fact holds those beliefs. If this conception is correct, only two tasks remain for explicit and possibly professional philosophical reasoning: first, to analyze and to understand the constitution of the moral image as it emerges with the moral viewpoint itself; second, to justify morality and the moral image against the charge that they can only be illusory. This justification would always have to address both moral consciousness and the moral image of the world at once.

This distinction is as interesting as it is important. It directly affects the way in which philosophy is related to ordinary life and the knowledge built into ordinary life prior to all theorizing. If the second account is correct, one must conclude that an ordinary person already possesses a kind of metaphysics, which philosophy can only understand and defend, or destroy—without being able to provide an equivalent. We should also note that there is a close connection between the second account of the moral image on the one hand and Kant's epistemology on the other. The transcendental approach to knowledge presupposes an indissoluble connection between the self-relatedness of the knower and a particular conception of a world of objects. Viewed according to the second model, a similar connection holds between the conscience of the moral agent and his moral image of the world. It thus makes sense to say that Rousseau's reasoning about the moral image is also the predecessor of Kant's epistemology—which is Rousseauian in spirit anyway.

I cannot, however, claim that Kant clearly distinguished between the two accounts of the connection between morality and the moral image, let alone that he did so at the time when Rousseau began to inspire him. The way Rousseau arrives at belief in the immortality of the soul fits better into the first account, whereas his argument that conscience presupposes the order of accord suggests or even requires the latter account. By contrast, in the course of his sketches for a moral theology, Kant comes ever closer to the second account. Eventually he first produces it with some clarity in the *Critique of Practical Reason*. He himself never regarded the distinction as a problem of first priority; it was Fichte who assessed it in this way. But Fichte had been exposed to numerous objections to Kant's moral theology, objections he tried to defeat by showing that Kant's thought can only be understood as an analysis of what is always already conceived of by the moral agent, whereas philosophers had lacked the tools and skills to disclose the ordinary person's and mind's world.

Instead, the problem with Rousseau that had troubled Kant from the very beginning was the following. Within the profession of faith Rousseau argues somewhat in the style of Descartes. He tries to secure propositions we cannot possibly negate. He uses conscience rather than consciousness as his fixed point. This procedure results in a number of theorems and articles of faith that are poorly connected to one another. But Kant had been educated within Leibniz's school. Thus a theoretical network whose consistency and completeness could be ascertained appeared to him as an unavoidable requirement for philosophical insight. In addition, Rousseau's talk of moral consciousness had been derived from British theories about the "Moral Sense." Kant sympathized with Hutcheson, who had shown the irreducibility of the moral perspective, but he also believed that morality cannot possibly be understood as originating from a particular sense. Rather, one must aim at understanding how it results from a distinctive and irreducible usage of reason. Rousseau—this time as the author of the *Social Contract*—encouraged such a view. The "general will" is obviously a rational principle. If it is valid within the philosophy of law, it should have at least an analogue in the philosophy of moral conduct. After all, even in *Emile*, Rousseau emphasizes the active nature of the human mind to an extent that makes his reference to the immediacy of conscience an archaic stranger in his discourse.

Consequently, Kant began to investigate possibilities of understanding the origination of the moral viewpoint through which the emergence of the moral image of the world would become comprehensible simultaneously and on the same grounds. His accomplishments and failures along this way led him eventually, rather late and via many shifts, to the doctrine shared by the *Critique of Practical Reason* and the *Critique of Judgment*.

Before turning to two stages on Kant's troublesome way, we should briefly attend to a dimension of Kant's thinking that continuously influences his reasoning within his moral theology: his analysis of the traditional notion of God. Kant's first *Critique* leads, among so many other things, to the insight that traditional ontology had been entirely misguided in its estimation of the order and usage of various fundamental notions. Where one used to conceive of these notions as a continuum specifying the notion "being," Kant discerns a variety of origins and usages. Thus, for instance, the concept of causality, the concept of identity, and the notion of the infinite differ completely in status and in origin. Before Kant arrived at these results, he had already applied the same method to the notion of God. This notion can only be understood as the result of a complicated, although rational, synthesis of a number of notions with different origins. It contains the notion of a *necessary* being. Yet taken by itself this notion would never issue in the singularity of God. It contains also the notion of a supreme or most perfect being. But this idea does not imply the necessity of God's existence. Most importantly, although our notion of God contains God's personhood, there is no way of convincing us on rational grounds that the necessary or the infinitely perfect being must possess a reason and a will. All our knowledge about reason and will depends upon familiarity with our own will and reason, which are marked by our finitude in a way that precludes the idea of their being increased to the degree of infinity. They are, to be sure, distinctive, real properties. But to the infinite being we can only attribute infinite properties. Consequently, we must conceive of reason and will as secondary, derivative perfections—an ever-viable way of accommodating them. Because this is possible, we have no decisive reason for attributing to the infinite being a mind and a will of a totally different and thus totally incomprehensible kind.

For obvious reasons, Kant didn't allow this tenet to surface fully in his texts. But he clearly proclaims that only via the reasoning of *moral* theology can one arrive at the notion of a personal God. Speculative theology doesn't rule it out, but is unable to lead to it. Speculative theology doesn't even indicate it, as Kant remarks in the *Critique of Pure Reason*. Pursuing this line of reasoning, he remarks that the notion of God analyzed in the philosophical tradition as the summit of the achievements of speculative reason originated from the very pure conception of the moral life in our religion.

This puts Kant's concern with the moral image of the world in yet another perspective. By understanding this image, he could hope to understand in greater depth the way in which the various usages of reason cooperate. They eventually arrive at conceptions by means of which what appears to be, and indeed is, divergent at the beginning reveals itself as belonging to an architectonic design—a design within which the rationality (and the conditions for the reality) of the moral life functions as the keystone.

I have already pointed out that the encounter with Rousseau induced Kant definitely to adopt positions other than moral theology as the best approach to philosophical theology at large. Two of them have been important for his subsequent reconstruction of moral theology. First, he adopted the conviction that all rational discourses must be analyzed as resulting from the employment of *activities*. He soon distinguished between the activity of the "intellect" and the activity of "reason." The former organizes our knowledge of objects given by intuition. By contrast, the latter projects ideas of a "maximum" or an "utmost limit"—either the limit of a sequence of causes, grounds, and underlying entities, or the maximum of an order. Second, he used his new analysis of what an "idea" consists in by applying it to the order of conduct. This resulted in the discovery of the categorical-imperative procedure: if everyone's actions and intentions could be such that the principles guiding them could be adopted by everyone else, and if everyone's will could always approve such an order without running into a contradiction, a maximum order within each individual will, as well as within all wills, would be established. In this way, Kant arrived at one of the fundamental theorems of his ethics.

But Kant had learned too much from the Moral Sense school to believe that with this move alone his ethics could come to its completion. A moral philosophy must always produce—in addition to the principle that effectively distinguishes morally good from morally bad—an account of the motivation of disinterested actions. But the more rational the principle of discerning the good becomes, the more difficult it will be to understand the motivation of the will that complies with the rational demand to act in the disinterested, moral way. Kant rated this problem so difficult and at the same time so important that he referred to it as "the philosophers' stone."

We can now turn to Kant's first explanation of the moral image of the world. He never published this theory, although it is highly original. It had been attractive to him for many years because, if it could be defended against all objections, it would solve three problems at once: (1) it would explain the origination of the moral principle itself, that is to say, the categorical imperative; (2) it would provide an explanation of moral motivation; and (3) it would show how the moral image of the world is connected with the moral principle. I shall give a brief survey of this as yet little-known theory, in eleven steps.

1. We have many needs and desires we cannot possibly relinquish. They not only differ from but also conflict with one another. We pursue them in various ways and to various degrees, possibly with prudence, inevitably with continuously changing preferences and postponements.

2. This situation is unsatisfactory for a rational agent. Hav-

ing the idea of a maximum at his disposal, he must apply this idea to his needs and desires. Thus the idea of a maximum satisfaction arises: the idea of *happiness*.

3. We cannot avoid striving for happiness. Yet at the same time we cannot even conceive of realizing this idea. There is no conceivable state within which, for instance, maximal peace and maximal excitement would coexist.

4. The inescapable adoption of this idea leads to much greater disorder than we experienced in the first place. Henceforth, we cannot avoid connecting with the pursuit of particular desires the hope that this will lead us to happiness. Because we also know that the hope will be thwarted, we shift to other (always futile) projections of happiness, albeit possibly in a daily routine.

5. Our reason must become deeply discontented with such a situation, because applying the idea of a maximum order resulted in an increase of *dis*order within our conduct. The idea of happiness originated from reason, but it caused a state opposite to what reason always intends to accomplish.

6. In such a situation, the idea of order must be applied once more. But this time it projects the idea of a kind of conduct that is necessarily released from all disorder, a maximum accordance among all imaginable actions, without taking into account particular interests and desires. This is the idea of the *moral law*.

7. The moral law imposes a condition upon all our striving for happiness. It cannot, however, amount to abandoning the hope for happiness, for both ideas arise from reason as such. Consequently the demand of the moral law is only that we suspend our hope for happiness whenever we meet situations to which the moral law applies. Furthermore, we must conceive of happiness in such a way that it cannot be attained unless the moral law has been fulfilled.

8. Given the internal connection between the moral law

and the idea of happiness, it follows that the moral law confirms the legitimacy of the hope for happiness. Hence it also implies the promise that this hope will be fulfilled, to the degree to which we meet the moral law's demands.

9. This enables us to accept our situation, namely, that we cannot even imagine in what our happiness could possibly consist. Our hope will now be directed toward an order beyond our knowledge—toward another dimension of our lives. Of it we know only that it must be a realm where a deity guarantees the appropriate distribution of happiness and moral merit. We have thus arrived at the *moral image.*

10. But we have simultaneously arrived at an understanding of the motivation of good will. The fulfillment of the moral law is the *only* way in which our unrenounceable hope for happiness could be realized—albeit in a way we cannot conceive of. This is the strongest motive we can imagine.

11. Yet it is not a motive of calculated self-interest, for we know nothing about the way in which we might eventually attain happiness. We have to meet the demands of the moral law and trust its promise in the first place.

To those familiar with Kant's published moral philosophy, it may come as a surprise that this is a Kantian theory. But clearly it is powerful and provides solutions to many urgent problems through a single chain of conclusions.

Rarely does a philosopher who possesses a theory of this kind silently abandon it. Kant began to withdraw from his first moral theology well before the publication of the *Critique of Pure Reason*. He replaced it with what we can describe as an intermediate theory, which preserved many features of its predecessor; traces of this intermediate theory can be found at a number of places in the concluding chapters of the first *Critique*. The definitive rejection must have taken place during the preparation of Kant's first book on moral philosophy, the *Groundwork of the Metaphysics of Morals* (1785). Here we cannot explore the reasons why Kant abandoned the theory that we can call "the theory of the worthiness of happiness." To dismantle its scaffolding and to point out the reasons for its failure would be a good exercise for a student of Kantian ethics. But Kant's mature theory indicates clearly what must have become a major source of his dissatisfaction: the theory suffers from a number of ambiguities, primarily within its account of moral motivation. On the one hand, it imposes a condition upon every hope for happiness that requires abstraction from all sensual interests, but on the other hand, it derives all the moral law's motivating power from the hope for happiness. It also intends to derive the rationality of the belief in God and the moral order from the validity of the moral law. Yet, by contrast, it makes this validity depend in part on the very same belief.

Once Kant had seen through these ambiguities, he was ready for a radical change in the basic design of his ethics: a moral philosophy worthy of the name must adopt as its point of departure the tenet that actions can only have a moral value if their motivation derives from the moral law alone. This insight led to Kant's well-known theory of "respect for the law" as the only moral motivation (a theory that cannot be explained as the result of a pietistic education, but only as the conclusion of a long process of reasoning). Its adoption resulted in a reconstruction of Kant's ethics in its entirety, indeed in much more, namely, in a new conception of the moral image of the world and in a new shape for the philosophical system at large.

The design of this new system includes the acknowledgment that "respect for the law" is a primordial motivation. It is impossible to derive it from other impulses or desires, or even from reason in general. Instead, it derives directly from awareness of the validity of the law. This implies that the principle of practical reason cannot be reduced to reason as the source of the idea of a maximum. The general structure of reason underlies, yet does not issue, the moral law. In precisely this sense the law is a "fact of reason." The insights that the validity of the law is a fact and that the only moral motive is respect for the law fit in well with the contention, backed up by the first *Critique*, that morality is the only manifestation and actualization of the freedom of the will. We lack any means of providing a proof of this particular kind of freedom, hence it can only manifest itself by itself. Consequently, the need for a defense of the belief in freedom cannot be met in any direct way. One can only show that this belief connects perfectly well with all proofs reason can provide and with all other convictions reason supports in one way or another. Taken together with the result that we cannot even expect that a proof of freedom might be possible, this way of arguing provides us with the only imaginable and thus satisfactory defense.

All this dramatically alters the view of the overall structure of reason, as well as of the way in which philosophy advances its insight and connects its disciplines. Philosophy cannot derive theorems from highest and self-evident premises. It must instead advance by investigating the connections between relatively independent domains of discourse. Since all these connections eventually indicate the reality of the principle from which moral conduct emerges, a comprehensive moral philosophy constitutes the conclusion of, rather than an application within, the system of philosophy.

Until he had arrived at this conception, Kant could not possibly have conceived of a *Critique of Judgment*. The book as a whole is shaped as a partial discipline within philosophy as an *ascent*. The very notion of a reflective judgment is the notion of an ascending power of the mind. And its other key term, the notion of purposefulness, is applied in an ascending manner, too: the *Critique of Judgment* begins with particu-

lar kinds of purposefulness, like the beautiful and the orga-
nism; it proceeds to nature as a teleological system and
arrives at the moral image of the world. In addition, the book
is conceived as a network of theories that connect our basic
knowledge about the laws constituting the empirical world
with the ultimate ideas of reason, and it provides an orderly
transition from the former to the latter. Before the revolution
in Kant's thought that led to the second *Critique*, the third *Critique* would not have been a possible candidate for a component of the philosophical system.

We now must return to the moral image of the world.
Kant's account of it obviously had to be modified once he had
abandoned the "theory of the worthiness of happiness." But
this change could not consist only in revising the explanation
of the moral image. Kant's conception of the way in which the
moral image is joined to the moral point of view also had to
be revised, for his new moral philosophy must be traced directly to the exclusion of any role happiness might play
within the motivation of the agent. Respect is the only motivation of the good will. So why does the agent need a moral
image of the world at all?

Kant could not possibly answer this question in the negative. He was too deeply convinced of the correctness of Rousseau's vision. Thus he promptly produced a new joint between the good will and the moral image: the moral law
demands a particular kind of conduct. But to act always
means to pursue *purposes*. Hence the moral agent pursues
purposes that derive from the good will. He attempts to help
other human beings and he aims to improve the overall condition of society so that evil will no longer flourish or just men
suffer. And since he simply cannot follow the law's demand
without believing that it is possible to succeed in all these re-
gards, he accepts, together with the validity of the moral law,
a view of what the world is like: its constitution must be such

that its effects are not indifferent to, or even counteract, morally motivated actions. This belief is a necessary implication
of the agent's moral conduct, whether he becomes aware of it
or not. It amounts, however, to assuming the existence of a
moral order such that a final purpose of the moral effort can
be arrived at. Moral actions that we believe always would
cause harm or worsen the condition of society would be self-
stultifying. Hence we can attribute to the good will a moral
image of the world, regardless of what the moral agent might
be able or willing to assert.

Kant points out clearly that belief in the existence of such
an order must be distinguished from a belief in God's existence. Yet he also claims that we cannot imagine a way of accounting for the existence of this order that does not have recourse to a supreme rational will. Thus he arrives again at the
same moral image. Yet this time it is not founded upon the
agent's own hope for happiness, but only on the agent's belief
that it is possible to promote a state of the world such that
merit and happiness are distributed in some way that is not
in open conflict with moral principles.

This account of the moral image became Kant's official doctrine. It is stated in the *Critique of Practical Reason* for the first
time. It also prevails in the *Critique of Judgment*. It is, indeed,
immune to charges that, thus conceived, a moral image still
depends on covert interests of the agent that are not exclusively moral. Kant can also avoid the objection that the moral
image is nothing but a helpful fiction the agent needs in order
to persuade himself of the reality of the moral law. For the
image arises spontaneously, together with the good will, and
cannot be separated from it. The theory is thus clearly supe-
rior to Kant's prior attempts to solve the problem posed by
Rousseau.

The new account suffers, however, from another weakness. And a few symptoms within the *Critique of Judgment* in-

dicate that Kant soon became aware of it. When Kant had arrived at his mature ethics of the "respect for the moral law" that is a "fact of reason," he swiftly redesigned his moral theology, and he could indeed be pleased with the results. He employed as the key instrument for the redesigning the notion of a "final purpose" of our actions, for only such a final purpose would enable him to reestablish a moral image with the same content as the preceding theory of the "worthiness of happiness"—while excluding from consideration the agent's own personal interest. But Kant took little pains to provide an analysis of the reasons that would justify his claim that every moral action must take place with regard to a final purpose of the world, which it must adopt as its ultimate perspective and objective. Yet such an analysis would have been mandatory because of the distinctive pattern of Kant's ethics itself: the moral law demands that all our actions must be of a particular *form*. The law as such remains totally indifferent to both the objectives and the outcomes of the actions of a will that adopts maxims meeting the requirement of universalizability. These maxims, to be sure, also constitute particular objectives. And Kant argues correctly that all moral conduct would collapse if we had to believe that all moral actions had effects that prevented their objectives' being actualized. Yet holding this and claiming that all moral actions jointly aim at a highest good in the world are clearly two different affairs.

Kant became aware of this gap in his argumentation fairly soon. He could not avoid noticing it because of the central complex of problems in the *Critique of Judgment* itself. The book's divergent subjects cohere in the investigation of the various uses of the notion of a purpose. Although Kant argued that these usages point to the notion of a final purpose, he could hardly overlook the need for an account of the source from which this notion is generated. It can, to be sure, emerge only within the moral context. But in precisely what way?

Kant doesn't address this question in the *Critique of Judgment.* He begins, however, to experiment with alternative strategies that might connect a moral image and the notion of God with the principle of his ethics. This does not mean that he began to suspect the notion of the final purpose as such. In fact, he never dispensed with it. But in the publications that succeeded the third *Critique* he disclosed in passing the new insight that he expressed in the basic language of transcendental philosophy: the connection between the notions of duty and the final purpose is a synthetic one. And because it takes place independently of experience, it is synthetic *a priori.* Hence the philosopher must meet the task of explaining the conditions of its possibility. In a note to the introduction of his book *Religion within the Limits of Reason Alone,* Kant also provides a key for solving the problem—yet with the remarkably reluctant qualification that it is a key only "to the extent to which I believe I understand the matter."

This marks the beginning of Kant's work on the moral image during his final decade. These efforts came to a standstill only within the last philosophical passages Kant could write. These lines, almost like the last brushstroke of a Zen master at the moment of his death, are related to the primary concern of his philosophy at large: the way in which a philosophical system can be built and completed, and the way in which it is related to the moral image of the world. But all this we must leave for another occasion.

Rousseau's and Kant's concern with the moral image of the world has exerted an enormous influence. It is one of the most important roots from which the entire spectrum of post-Kantian philosophy has grown. It inspired both Fichte and Hegel. Kierkegaard's notion of "existence," like Marx's notion of "ideology," can be traced back to it. But even that would not suffice to justify spending so much time with it. I think, however, that we, too, still have many reasons for investigating further what Kant pursued in his lifelong effort.

Anyone who finds modern physicalist materialism irresistibly strong must accept that all his personal life, including his conceptions of knowledge, proceeds within a network of indispensable illusions. Whoever thinks differently must know that an easy reconciliation between objective knowledge and the perspectives of the first-person viewpoint is not available. Only a subtle philosophy can possibly accommodate the latter in depth without eliminating it at the same time—perhaps involuntarily and only by implication.

That this is so can be explained to a considerable degree by the mutual dependences between self-interpretations of the First Person on the one hand, and images of the world on the other. Consequently, we cannot refrain from investigating these numerous connections, from relating them to one another, and from examining to what degree we are justified in accepting these perspectives as both irreducible and valid.

I believe that Kant was indeed ill-advised when, without hesitation, he identified the moral order with the order of the highest good and the realm of grace. But that by no means implies that the notion of a moral order can be dispensed with or that it is devoid of content. In addition, unlike Kant, we must distinguish between various kinds of moral conduct and stages within the development of the moral awareness of man. This adds yet another dimension to the notion of the moral image of the world. Hence, although our analyses have shown that Kant's books cannot be used as sources of everlasting insight, he did found a philosophical tradition and open up a philosophical perspective with which we can and should remain affiliated.

Kant's Explanation of Aesthetic Judgment

K A N T ' S *Critique of Judgment* is generally considered to be a turning point in the history of aesthetics and the philosophy of art. It combines and reconstructs the analyses of aesthetic predicates and the aesthetic attitude that emerged in Leibniz's and Locke's schools, as they have been formulated by philosophers like Alexander Baumgarten and Johann Georg Sulzer on the one hand and like Hume and Burke on the other. But it also elevated the aesthetic theory to a new level by integrating it into the framework of a new epistemology that Kant had worked out in the *Critique of Pure Reason* based on the view that what we call "reason" consists in a complex interaction of various epistemic operations. To understand what "reason" accomplishes, one must look for operations from which such accomplishments arise. In addition, one must look to the sources from which these operations originate and to the principles or rules that guide them. The *Critique of Judgment* discloses such a source for the appreciation of the beautiful (and the sublime). Thus it proved possible to separate aesthetic judgments from other types of judgments while preserving their claim to originate in reason as such and from activities that are interwoven with the activities on which all knowledge of our world depends. These judgments, to be sure, don't express knowledge. But their claim is justified because it is founded upon the same activities from which knowledge originates, albeit in a distinctive, interactive employment. Hence Kant first provided tools for establishing the aesthetic attitude as self-contained and autonomous, thus as the foundation for a conception of art that envisages art as a primordial way of being related to and situated within our world, a way that can neither be replaced nor surpassed by other achievements of man's rational capacities.

This is how the *Critique of Judgment* has been perceived by the philosophers and theoreticians of art who succeeded Kant. The result Kant arrived at became an almost unquestioned premise of subsequent endeavors within aesthetics, up to our own time.

This brief outline of Kant's accomplishment does not correctly describe Kant's own intention, however. He wrote the *Critique of Judgment* because he aimed to complete what he called his "critical business"—the investigation of all knowledge claims involving principles that cannot be justified by experience alone. Because earlier metaphysics had failed, it had become indispensable to understand the origins of knowledge claims, as the only means by which one could distinguish real knowledge from deeply rooted illusions. Because of the novelty and the difficulties of such an investigation, Kant believed that one could not rely on particular results before they were confirmed and supported by results in other areas of knowledge where a priori principles apparently also come into play. This methodologically holistic conviction implies that critical philosophy can establish itself decisively only as a *system*. And because many of the most important types of rational discourse cannot be reduced to one single fundamental mode of employing reason, the critical system could only adopt the form of a systematic connection of relatively self-contained discourses—an architectural structure that might (as Kant believed) eventually reveal a "highest point" made possible and supported by all the other discourses—which is (according to Kant) the consciousness of human freedom.

In this way, we can explain why Kant felt that he had to write a "Critique of Taste" when he had arrived at the insight that aesthetic judgment cannot be understood without including the claim that it is valid for every rational being of our kind, a claim that can be based neither upon experience nor upon rational proof, which would amount to saying that a distinctive a priori principle must be involved. Consequently—given Kant's methodological conviction—a critical investigation became mandatory.

This might sound as though Kant turned to the subject of aesthetics almost involuntarily, and not for its own sake. One might then easily suspect that he had been ill-prepared for an analysis of the subtle and complex facts with which aesthetics must come to terms. One might even be tempted to admire Kant's genius because of his ability to compose such a rich and attractive work on aesthetic phenomena from a point of view and an interest exclusively consumed in the task of completing the system of transcendental philosophy.

But this assessment of Kant's preparation for designing an aesthetics is grossly inadequate. Kant had been thinking over its topics and problems for decades. In 1764, he had published the essay "Observations on the Feeling of the Beautiful and the Sublime." In the course of his lectures, he frequently discussed aesthetic problems. His government required that lecture courses use printed textbooks as guidelines. Kant (who held a chair of logic and metaphysics) used in his annually repeated public courses textbooks by two leading aestheticians of his time: Meier's *Logic* and Baumgarten's *Metaphysics*. The logic Kant wanted to teach had a much broader scope than that taught in contemporary logic courses. Kant described it as an instruction of the ordinary intellect as it borders, on the one side upon ignorance and, on the other, upon science and scholarship. Meier's textbook appeared to suit this purpose comparatively well. But within its treatment of the various kinds of knowledge it included such topics as the difference between a logical and an aesthetic perfection of knowledge and between a logical, an aesthetic, and a practical truth. It is therefore hardly surprising that we find elaborate reports of Kant's views on aesthetics in transcripts of his logic courses.

Kant gave his logic course every summer. During the winter, he lectured on metaphysics out of Baumgarten. The third of Baumgarten's book's four parts contains, as an indispensable prerequisite for the doctrines of metaphysical psychology, Baumgarten's "psychologia empirica." Here we find definitions in Wolff's spirit of the powers and the activities of the mind. Kant must have known this text by heart, and we can assume that he presupposes it as a stock of general knowledge when he introduces his own conceptual apparatus in the key chapters of the *Critique of Pure Reason*. Yet Baumgarten's text also contains discussions of mental capacities and states that are of obvious importance within aesthetics. It also contains frequent references to the philosophical discipline "aesthetica" and to the first book to carry this title, which had been published by Baumgarten himself.

Within his lectures on metaphysics Kant devoted only minimal attention to Baumgarten's empirical psychology, but not because he assigned little importance to it. Instead, he had developed another (and this time private) lecture course under the title "Anthropology," which he also gave every winter. These lectures were *exclusively* based on the "psychologia empirica" of Baumgarten's textbook. Consequently, we can take for granted that Kant had to discuss problems of aesthetics and present his views on this subject twice each winter to different audiences.

Therefore it is no surprise that Kant had developed his own aesthetics before he came to terms with the problems he intended to solve in the *Critique of Pure Reason*. Although the numerous transcripts of his anthropology lectures still await publication, we can already design a sufficiently accurate picture of Kant's earlier aesthetics, because Kant's own notes on Baumgarten and Meier, on which he based his lectures, have been preserved. The transcripts of the lectures on logic and metaphysics have also been published. What is really surprising is the extent to which this aesthetics coincides with the theorems of the *Critique of Judgment*. Almost all the notions the third *Critique* employs had been used by Kant in approximately the same sense fifteen years earlier.

To mention a few, Kant explains the aesthetic attitude as resulting from a "harmonious play" of our mental faculties in general and of the active sources of our cognition, imagination, and understanding in particular. He also remarks that judgment is operative within this play and provides it with its true unity, whereby the playful activity is strengthened in turn. The play results in pleasure. And this pleasure of "taste" differs from the pleasures of the senses because it originates from an activity; it is disinterested because it has as its object only formal properties of what is given in intuition. Kant also distinguishes clearly between the agreeable, which pleases particular subjects in changeable conditions, the beautiful, which pleases everybody universally, and the good, which is approved on rational grounds and gives rise to pleasure only in various indirect ways.

Yet Kant still persistently denied that the philosophical discipline of aesthetics could be founded upon a priori principles. One of the arguments with which he backs up this position is the lack of rules for taste. We could, to be sure, produce some such rules (e.g., order, proportion, symmetry, and harmony). But these rules are in turn founded upon our experience of what we take to be beautiful. They cannot be justified by reason alone. This argument would be consistent with the position of the *Critique of Judgment*, which also excludes rules of taste for which one could pretend to provide a rational justification. Consequently Kant's decisive argument must have been this: we cannot detect reasons why the harmonious play of our cognitive faculties arises as it does and in the circumstances that it does. It simply occurs. Therefore the occurrence of that play can only be a fact of the natural constitution of human cognition. Its description must be given within "psychologia empirica" in the strict sense, from which it follows that aesthetics must be conceived as an ultimately empirical discipline. Within this discipline we can account for the special status of aesthetic judgment and thus for the fact that it assumes the possibility of a universal agreement, and therefore for the further fact that we become engaged in disputes about the beautiful, although we refrain from such disputes in matters where the pleasure arises from sensation.

This was precisely the argument Kant abandoned when he conceived of writing a critique of taste that would correspond to what the preceding two *Critiques* accomplished with regard to theoretical and practical reason. When he rethought the epistemology of the *Critique of Pure Reason* he quickly saw that his epistemological theorems about the relationship between imagination and understanding would allow him to produce an explanation of aesthetic judgment whose sources would not be empirical throughout but rather derived from the explanation of the possibility of our knowledge of objects. Hence the new explanation would have the a priori status of a transcendental insight.

We can now understand why Kant felt he could carry out

his plan, once conceived, with little trouble. Most of the content of his aesthetics had been available to him for a long time. Its views and its conceptual apparatus of the cognitive activities had only to be transferred to a new context. Even the prior description of the distinctive features of aesthetic judgment could be maintained. All along he had noticed that these judgments claim universal agreement and a validity that cannot be supported by decisive reasons. By now he found himself in the position to justify this claim.

This doesn't amount to saying that Kant's earlier aesthetics remained entirely unchanged. Yet the change consisted less in additions to the theorems and innovations within the terminology than in a greater precision in their employment. Previously, Kant's reference to a harmonious play of our cognitive faculties had been somewhat vague and flexible. The paradigmatic case of an object that occasions this heightened and harmonious activity had been for Kant the work of art, which indeed engages perception, imagination, judgment, and thoughtful reflection at the same time. In the new "Critique of Taste" (which was soon extended to the project of a *Critique of Judgment*) the notion of the play of the faculties received a more restricted and precise meaning. From now on the only activities engaged in the play were the very activities shown by the *Critique of Pure Reason* to be operative in the constitution of objects from given intuitions in space and time. Consequently, natural objects and products of the skilled crafts had to be moved into the position of paradigm cases of the beautiful, while the work of art became the subject of a complex theory with a richer set of premises. At the same time and for the same reason, the harmonious play was moved closer to the perceptual process and thus, as Kant expressed himself, deeper into the depth of the mind—a change one can hardly deplore, for an aesthetics that commences with a theory of art always proceeds on insecure ground and through unexplored territory.

If one had to name a single component of the doctrines of the *Critique of Pure Reason* as the means by which Kant could integrate his aesthetics into his epistemology, it would have to be Kant's analysis of the various functions of *imagination* within cognition. In a note to the "Deduction" chapter of the original edition of the first *Critique*, Kant remarks proudly that no psychologist so far has conceived of the idea that imagination might be a necessary ingredient of perception itself (A 120).

A perception is a cognitive state in which a sensible manifold is present to us in a particular combination. Kant believes he has arguments to the effect that no combination can be given to us through the senses. Each combination has to be established through a cognitive operation for which the potentials of our imagination are responsible. Because perception is the elementary conscious state in cognition, we are led to the conclusion that imagination is operative, at least in part, before consciousness can arise. Kant employs this theorem in many contexts, but primarily in his analysis of how the notion of an object has to be understood and of how a world of objects is constituted for us through the activities of our understanding.

Kant holds that the exertion of our imagination is not self-contained. Imagination is the source of all combinations within what is sensibly given to us. But one cannot combine—at least one cannot combine a manifold into the structure of an object—unless principles of unity can be presupposed that guide the combinatory activity and determine its objective. Hence imagination in its most important cognitive usage depends upon pure concepts of an object that originate from our understanding—concepts that are at the same time the indispensable conditions for the possibility of the thought of oneself as a constant and unchangeable point of reference for all one's thoughts and judgments.

This brief summary of Kant's well-known tenets regarding the relationship between imagination and understanding helps us elucidate the difficulties an interpretation of Kant's explanation of aesthetic judgment has to face. For it reminds us of the basic design of the epistemology that, according to Kant, allowed and indeed necessitated the move from an ultimately empirical aesthetics to an aesthetics founded upon transcendental principles. When Kant speaks in the *Critique of Judgment* of a harmonious play between imagination and understanding, he clearly appeals to his account of the two cognitive capacities as they had been analyzed in the *Critique of Pure Reason*.

In cognition and in the formation of knowledge, the two faculties necessarily cooperate, but certainly not in a harmonious play that would require the two players to operate independently of each other. Rather, imagination here thoroughly depends upon understanding and serves, so to speak, its purposes. Yet in the brief formative period of the *Critique of Judgment*, Kant convinced himself that there can be and indeed must be another way in which the operations of the two capacities are coordinated. Imagination can correspond spontaneously to a requirement established by the understanding. This correspondence would, in turn, facilitate the understanding's business and thus strengthen and expand its own operations. Furthermore, the state within which this interaction would occur could not possibly be a case of an employment of a concept, for that would inevitably amount to still another case where the imagination could only serve rather than support freely the understanding's objective. Hence one has to conceive of a cooperation between the faculty of combination (imagination) and the faculty of con-

cepts (understanding) that takes place *prior* to the employment of any particular concept.

From this image of a distinctive way in which the most fundamental cognitive capacities cooperate Kant's new theory of
aesthetic judgment benefits in many ways. To begin with,
aesthetic judgments are singular judgments; they are asserted while we are exposed to an individual object or scene
in a perceptual situation. And we can assert these judgments
without having a description of the object at our disposal.
This is readily explained in terms of a cognitive process that
takes place in close proximity to the process of perceiving and
that precedes the process of concept formation in principle
although it is compatible with it. Furthermore, because aesthetic judgment cannot be based on the usage of concepts,
the reason for its being asserted can only be the occurrence of
a distinctive state of feeling about the object or scene within a
perceptual situation. This feeling in turn can be explained as
resulting from the animation and the quickening of imagination and understanding in their harmonious play. In this way
Kant eventually was able to arrive at a stable relationship between well-defined concepts of imagination, understanding,
play, and feeling—a stability that was lacking in his earlier
aesthetics.

That the play of the cognitive operations he envisaged had
to be located so close to the perceptual process, such that the
result of their coordinated interaction could only be revealed
through a feeling, did not raise difficulties from Kant's point
of view. His theory of perception requires anyway an employment of understanding that precedes judging and every conscious use of concepts. Kant's model of the foundation of aesthetic judgment includes, to be sure, a further component:
not only is the harmonious play simply a fact that takes place
in the depth of the mind; it also depends intrinsically on the
noticing of the mutual accordance of the operations of imagi-

nation and understanding. Kant claims that the noticed accordance is what results in a quickened activity. Thus one might suspect that he has to take recourse to a cognitive accomplishment that cannot possibly precede, and result in nothing but, a feeling. But this suspicion would be misguided. For Kant has at his disposal the notion of another mental activity, which Wolff and his school had analyzed under the name of "reflection." Reflection belongs (together with attention) to the most elementary employments of the intellect. It is a form of knowledge that intrinsically accompanies the operations of the mind and helps to keep them within their distinctive boundaries. This results in the possibility of a *comparison* of the states and accomplishments of operations that are connected to and entangled with one another. Reflection and comparison so conceived can take place (and must take place in many cases) independently of any explicit awareness. This notion of reflection has become totally alien to us, whereas Kant employs many variants of it and evidently assumes it is familiar to everybody. (It should be noted in passing that reflection has to be distinguished from reflective judgment, and that when Kant speaks of reflection as functioning in the process of concept formation, this is still another of the term's many employments.)

To sum up, we can by now understand why Kant became convinced that his epistemology provides all the resources for an explanation of aesthetic judgment that would at the same time elucidate and justify its claim to universal agreement. The objective of a critique had been defined by Kant as the justification of such a claim by means of an elucidation of the conditions of its possibility. He found himself by now in a position to account for these conditions. Consequently, he believed that the justification had been accomplished. This explains why his reasoning within the *Critique of Judgment* frequently takes the form of an argument the first premise for which is the fact that the claim of universal agreement is inevitably connected with aesthetic judgment: since the claim can only be explained by means of his account of the harmonious play, it *must* be this distinctive state of our cognitive faculties upon which aesthetic judgment is founded.

Such a stance, however, with regard to the fundamental problem of aesthetics can hardly satisfy us as long as the principal tool of Kant's account remains insufficiently exposed and explained: the structure of the harmonious play. One could very well describe the fabrication of this tool as a combination of an old idea, that of the animation of the mind in a playful activity, with the new theory of the synthetic activities of the mind. This description makes mandatory our efforts to ascertain that the combination results in both a structure free of tensions and a plausible image of the epistemic state expressed through aesthetic judgment.

The text of the third *Critique* accomplishes very little, indeed almost nothing, in this regard. Kant repeatedly uses his phrase "the play between imagination and understanding." He also characterizes the states of the two operations that are engaged in the play in various ways. The most frequent and significant characterization describes the play of the imagination as free and contrasts it with the activity of the understanding "in its lawfulness." But all this doesn't lead us very far and remains unacceptably metaphorical, for the phrase and its various extensions are unsupplemented by further analyses and illustrations clarifying precisely how the cognitive operations take place and *can* take place in the way envisaged. Kant himself was not insensitive to the weaknesses of his expositions. In the Preface (the latest part of the manuscript) we find a confession, which is certainly rare in Kant's work: "Here [in the inquiry into our power of taste], given how difficult it is to solve a problem that nature has made so involved, I hope to be excused if my solution contains a certain amount of obscurity, not altogether avoidable, as long as I have established clearly enough that the principle has been stated correctly" (1st ed., pp. ix–x).

There is only one further place where Kant made a similar confession, this time concerning the first edition of the transcendental deduction. But in that case he announced at the same time a forthcoming improved version of his text and its argument, which he indeed published soon afterwards, whereas he never rewrote parts of the *Critique of Judgment* in subsequent editions. Moreover, other writings and manuscripts betray scant evidence of a continuous effort on Kant's part. Apparently, Kant felt unable to proceed much further and imputed this to the matter's being "so involved."

Such a situation clearly challenges the interpreter to exercise both exegetical and philosophical skills. He cannot hope to find passages in Kant by means of which to clarify the philosopher's thoughts and intentions decisively. On the other hand, Kant by no means gives him permission just to repeat or vary his own phrases. An argumentative analysis is not only welcome but definitely required—an analysis that explores the theoretical and argumentative potentials at Kant's disposal. Only thus can one come up with a reading of the basic theorem in Kant's aesthetics that is both Kantian in nature and an improvement upon Kant's own expositions, which he himself admitted to be unsatisfactory.

A survey of the secondary literature rapidly reveals that the challenge is only sometimes understood and nowhere met. The task is difficult, requiring a mobilization of all the resources of Kant's epistemology. For although Kant did admit that his own "inquiry into our power of taste" remained obscure, he certainly believed that it fits perfectly into the complex doctrine of the interaction between imagination and understanding that he had worked out in the epistemology of his *Critique of Pure Reason*. In what follows I shall present and put up for discussion a solution of the problem.

When Kant admitted that his inquiry remained obscure, he probably had in mind two theorems that jointly constitute the third *Critique*'s innovation over his earlier aesthetics. First, the theorem of the harmonious play of imagination and understanding, and second, the theorem about the way in which this harmonious state within cognition is revealed by a *feeling*. The second theorem raises serious difficulties too, for the feeling has to be such that there can be no doubt that the aesthetic attitude has occurred. Otherwise a distinctively aesthetic judgment could not be based upon it, let alone a judgment claiming universal agreement. I shall disregard the latter problem—which can be solved without taking into consideration Kant's epistemology at large—and investigate exclusively the theorem of the harmonious play.

Attempts to interpret Kant's theorem are easily led into impasses by the overall design of the *Critique of Judgment*. Such an impasse can result from the notion of the faculty of reflective judgment that underlies the aesthetic as well as the teleological part of the third *Critique*. Kant explains this notion by reference to the *acquisition*, as opposed to the *application*, of concepts or general terms: in one of its employments the power of judgment applies general terms to particular cases; as such it is "determinative" judgment. But we are frequently in situations that expose us to objects for which applicable general concepts are lacking. These situations call for the employment of "reflective" judgment, which searches for and develops the appropriate general concept. Aesthetic judgments are based upon a usage of reflective judgment.

One has, however, to be cautious not to apply this model without further consideration. It is intended to apply first to the search for properties shared in common by classes of objects in nature and thus to the attempt to arrive at a classification of and a generalization over natural phenomena and the laws of nature. This concern is obviously quite remote from the situation in which aesthetic judgments are entertained and asserted. The classification of nature is a goal-directed, deliberate activity, whereas aesthetic judgment can develop and be entertained spontaneously and independently of any deliberation and investigation.

We would equally be led astray if we modified the picture only by insisting that reflective judgment's search for concepts in the aesthetic situation must be the search for ordinary general concepts of the first order. This could easily commit us to the unwelcome conclusion that our reason for using the predicate "beautiful" *dissolves* as soon as a general concept is found that applies to the object in question. The aesthetic situation must be understood in a way that does not collide with an indisputable fact: aesthetic judgments are compatible with every conceivable way of classifying and theorizing over a given object—provided we are exposed to that object in a perceptual situation.

The basic design of Kant's aesthetics encompasses still another trap for the incautious. Kant substantiates the rightfulness of the claim to universal agreement on the part of aesthetic judgment with the contention that the harmonious interaction between imagination and understanding is a necessary condition of the possibility of empirical knowledge. If "condition" were read here in the strong sense of "prerequisite," it would follow either that every object of which we can possibly have knowledge has to be beautiful in the first place, or that we cannot arrive at any knowledge about objects unless we experience the beauty of *some* object at the same time. The second absurdity is only of a slightly lesser magnitude than the first one. Consequently both conclusions have to be avoided by all means. Yet to see this and to discern a viable escape from the impasses are obviously two quite different things.

So far our results have been negative, and they suggest that we cannot expect an easy solution to our problem. The Kantian model of the cognitive state upon which the aesthetic judgment is based appears to be somewhat complicated and subtle. We have good reason to look into Kant's epistemology more closely to discover the most promising point of departure for a theory that would provide the required background for Kant's talk about a harmonious play of imagination and understanding.

The power of judgment functions prominently in the *Critique of Pure Reason*, specifically in the chapter preceding the discussion of the principles of pure understanding—the chapter that expounds Kant's doctrine of the schematism. Since it also deals with the relationship between understanding and imagination, one suspects from the outset that Kant, at least in part, will allude to this doctrine when he connects his aesthetics with the foundations of his epistemology. But once again caution is in order, for two reasons.

In the first place, whatever the doctrine of the schematism amounts to in particular, it certainly employs the notion of the power of judgment in its *determinative* sense: concepts, that is to say the categories, are at our disposal; how they can be applied to particular instances of what is given in intuition is the question up for discussion. Yet reflective judgment operates in the *reverse* direction; and a usage of the power of judgment that moves from intuitions toward the *categories* cannot be conceived of precisely because the categories originate prior to and independently of all intuitions.

In the second place, imagination is responsible for the formation of perceptions. And since the origination of the aesthetic attitude is located by Kant in close proximity to the perceptual process, one has reason to suspect that it is somehow entangled with the process through which we originally become aware of objects in general. There is some truth in this. But again, any attempt to approximate the two processes without emphasizing their differences would lead to unacceptable results, for aesthetic judgment always presupposes that an object is given to us which we then judge to be beautiful. This judgment, assuredly, is based upon the perception of the object, and this feature of it has to be accounted for. But the operation or set of operations through which a world of given objects is disclosed to us and which gives all perceptions of objects in this world their distinctive formal constitution cannot be the very same process on which, in whatever way, the aesthetic judgment is based. For aesthetic judgments are individual judgments about particular objects within particular perceptual situations.

We have arrived at still another negative result. It leads us, however, to a conclusion that reduces the range of possible solutions to our problem: we cannot hope to render intelligible Kant's talk of the play between imagination and understanding as long as we interpret understanding as the power that employs the categories as unifying principles of the synthetic activity of imagination. Consequently, judgment that is reflective and thus in search of concepts has to be understood, first of all, as being in search of *empirical* concepts.

But now we have to be afraid of being pushed back into one of the impasses already discussed. In his lectures on logic Kant always expounded as his own the analysis Wolff had given of the formation of empirical concepts: we compare given objects, reflect upon what they have in common, and abstract this from the rest, whereupon what they have in common becomes the content of a concept that applies to the objects in question as well as to other objects. Here we encounter again the notion of reflection in one of its many usages. But we have already mentioned two reasons why aesthetic judgment cannot be understood as a preliminary stage on the way to the actual acquisition of empirical concepts. First, aesthetic judgments are and remain distinctive singular judgments; they can never be replaced by the application of descriptive concepts. Second and even more important, the situation in which they make sense doesn't include any comparison with other objects. But to compare is the first among the activities required for the formation of empirical concepts—according to Kant's teaching.

The situation has begun to look very much like a dilemma. One of its horns prevents any recourse to the relationship between imagination and a priori concepts (the categories). The other horn exposes us to the threat that any recourse to the only alternative, the formation of empirical concepts, is also condemned to failure. But although a model that projects the play of the powers upon the employment of the categories has been definitely excluded, we might still find a solution by using in a more sophisticated way a Kantian view of the formation of empirical concepts. Let us turn to such an attempt.

Kant wrote two versions of the Introduction to the *Critique of Judgment*. He discarded the first because it was too long and rewrote the entire text shortly before the book was printed. But the first Introduction had been written half a year earlier, while the problems of aesthetics discussed in the oldest portion of the work were much more vividly on Kant's mind. Thus it is no surprise that the first Introduction contains some clues to an adequate reconstruction of Kant's line of reasoning.

Kant substantiates here his contention that the play of the faculties takes place at the very beginning of the process of conceptualization by remarking that the aesthetic attitude arises "before we attend to a comparison of an object with others" (AA XX,224). But comparison is the first of the activities leading to the formation of empirical concepts. This amounts to saying that a process of reflection regarding the possible formation of concepts commences *before* any attempt has been made to discover what objects share. One cannot, of course, avoid wondering *in what way* the faculty of understanding can become involved and then operative in a sufficiently elementary manner in a situation thus conceived. To repeat: Kant describes the situation in which the harmonious play takes place with reference to imagination (whose operations he says are "free") *as well as* with reference to understanding, which he says is involved "in its lawfulness." We must, once again, wonder how understanding, in its lawfulness, can enter a situation that cannot be elucidated by reference to the constitutive usage of the categories and that precludes general concepts.

We have come to a turning point. Once one realizes that this is precisely the question that has to be answered, a solution of our problem can begin to emerge. That Kant himself must have envisaged such a solution can again be shown by means of passages from the first Introduction. The key term for the solution, which term Kant employs only here in a prominent way within the context of aesthetics, is "exhibition" ("Darstellung," traditionally translated as "presentation").

The introduction of this term into the language of philosophy is one of Kant's many accomplishments. He employs it in his theory of the *usage* of concepts. Although Kant's theory of the *acquisition* of concepts coincided with the traditional theory, he developed a rather advanced view on the *possession* and the *usage* of concepts. It derived from his central doctrine about the fundamental difference between intuition and concept and their mutual dependence within knowledge. Concepts without intuitions are not only empty in the well-known general sense of Kant's famous sentence, but also empty—or rather, not really in our possession—if we don't know how to apply them. But applying them means to be capable of producing instances of them in intuition. Instances can, to be sure, be produced in many ways; and the more abstract the concepts are the more difficult this will be. But Kant holds that ordinarily and ultimately instances have to be produced in intuition, whose unitary form is temporal and spatial. It is this context within which the term "exhibition" acquires its philosophical meaning. To exhibit a concept means to associate with it in intuition a manifold of a distinctive unitary (temporal and/or spatial) shape.

The only explicit exposition of the theorem is found in the chapter on the schematism. The objective of this chapter is the exhibition of the categories, thus concepts a priori. But it states clearly that the possession of empirical concepts includes the ability to exhibit them as well. The first Introduction, looking back to the analysis of taste, points out with equal clarity that the power of judgment holds up the imagination (as it merely apprehends the object) to the understanding (as it *exhibits* a concept in general) (AA XX,223). We are now in the position to illustrate Kant's metaphorical talk of the harmonious play in a way that sheds considerable light on the aesthetic experience.

But first I will briefly discuss a possible objection and a difficulty that might have prevented interpreters from achieving an adequate reading of Kant's critique of taste. One can object that although the "exhibition" of a quality like "red" can consist in the production of some red objects, Kant insists that in the aesthetic situation only formal—namely, spatial and temporal—features count. But then we have to remind ourselves that in the aesthetic situation no *particular* concept can be exhibited, for the absence of appropriate concepts is essential to it. If the understanding operates in the aesthetic situation as the power of exhibiting concepts, it must do so by virtue of a feature distinctive of the exhibition of concepts that are derived from perceptions in a general and formal way. This can only be the unity and the precision of the *arrangement* of a perceived manifold in space and time.

A further difficulty with the Kantian theory of the foundation of aesthetic judgment we are about to design seems to be this. The direction in which reflective judgment operates is *from* perception and imagination *toward* understanding and its concepts. But "exhibition" is, in contrast, a notion that has its place within the theory of the usage and the application of concepts. Thus it appears to be confined to the scope of the activity of determinative judgment; and that disqualifies it for any service in a Kantian aesthetics. The difficulty can strike one as very serious. It might even explain in part Kant's failure to present his view all along with reference to "exhibition" as the contribution of understanding to the aesthetic situation.

Nevertheless, the difficulty dissolves rapidly at this stage of our investigation, in the following way. It is reflective judgment that holds the power of imagination (as it perceives and thus synthesizes a manifold) up to the understanding. But that does not necessarily mean that it is engaged in a search for concepts that would actually apply to the perception in question. Rather, it compares the state of imagination with the conditions of a possible conceptualization in general. Yet a symptom of the possession of a concept is always the possibility of its being exhibited in intuition. One cannot even search for concepts unless one conceives them already in light of the way in which they can be exhibited. But that amounts to saying that the ascent of reflective judgment from imagination toward understanding necessarily always already takes into account the way in which concepts are generally applied and thus exhibited. This is precisely how understanding as such enters the play *prior* to the acquisition of any particular concept.

The picture of the harmonious play that begins to emerge has many attractive aspects for aesthetics. Kant links the aesthetic experience closely to the cognitive process. But he can still avoid its intellectualization. He is also able to account for both the complexity and the internal unity displayed by objects we describe as beautiful. Imagination provides the complexity, and the accordance with the general structure of exhibition provides the concise unity of the form. Both features can be encountered in perception as such. But their harmony is revealed only through the intellectual operation of reflection, which in turn continuously refers to what only the understanding can accomplish. It will be hard to find other aesthetic theories that could claim similar achievements.

But our account of the harmonious play is still incomplete, for we have not yet discussed how the *freedom* of imagination enters the picture. (Kant, one will remember, describes the harmonious play as taking place between imagination *in its freedom* and understanding in its lawfulness.) In its ordinary operation, imagination is by no means free. Rather, it *serves* other cognitive powers in various ways. (1) It synthesizes what is given in intuition according to the rules of understanding (the categories). (2) It apprehends particular manifolds while respecting the way in which the manifolds are given. (3) It provides instances of empirical concepts by designing appropriate images for them by means of which the concepts are "exhibited." What then does it mean that it operates freely?

To respond to this question, one can reason in the following way. A power suitable for such various service hardly depends completely upon one of the masters it serves or upon all of them jointly. It must have the potential to operate in a way both natural to itself and adaptable to many different functions. All the bound functions of imagination amount to the constitution of particular forms and shapes. Thus if the activity of imagination develops freely, it will pass through manifolds in various ways and produce traces of forms without aiming at particular forms and without stopping when they have been attained. The "fantasia" in music is thus not by accident named after an employment of imagination that, according to Kant, has a cognitive analogue or foundation. Kant followed Hobbes in analyzing *pleasure* as the heightened state, the *quickening* of an activity. Thus the free activity of imagination must be pleasing in itself.

This free activity, however, is not yet equivalent to the harmonious play of the cognitive powers. This play does not take place before the free employment of imagination results by itself in the creation of forms that correspond to the general feature of an exhibition of an empirical concept. In such cases the lawfulness of understanding is fulfilled without any coercion. And this, in turn, at least appears to facilitate the understanding's activity. It also strengthens the understanding's readiness to form concepts and to apply them, which means to exhibit them. Imagination profits from this accordance too. For the power of understanding refrains from further interference in such a situation. Rather, it accepts and approves the continuation of the free activity of its counterpart.

Moreover, one has to bear in mind that all this has to take place within a perceptual situation. Exhibition requires that the precise form of an empirical object will be produced. It may appear as if this would be incompatible with the freedom of imagination. But Kant claims correctly that it is quite conceivable that an object presents in perception precisely that form imagination would create while being engaged in its free activity. In addition, the very same form can suit the general features of an exhibition. Whenever all three of these conditions are fulfilled at the same time, the harmonious play originates. It results in the readiness of the mind to *contemplate* the object in question continuously—until the needs of the daily life or the tiring of the attention bring contemplation to an end. We describe such an object as beautiful.

The aesthetic state of the harmonious play is embedded in many other cognitive operations. (1) It is preceded by the constitution of a world of objects. The free performance of imagination accords with (2) the perception of a particular empirical object. (3) The understanding can entertain any knowledge with regard to the object it might possess. It would not disturb the aesthetic situation or contribute to it in any way.

But the power of reflective judgment is indeed constitutive of the situation. For only by virtue of reflection can the accordance of the accomplishments of the two powers be noticed. The power of imagination, to be sure, can remain free within its perceiving without any reference to understanding as such. But the heightened activity of understanding depends upon the noticing of the accordance of its own activity with the freedom of imagination.

The harmonious agreement of the cognitive powers, thus conceived, is playful in a particular sense: the mutual agreement comes about without coercion, and the two activities concur automatically. The play can thus be compared to a dance of two partners who harmonize in their movements without influencing each other and who enjoy their joint performance.

We must, however, admit that in the very few places where Kant does not speak only in abstraction about the play, he conceives it more frequently as an interaction. In that case a ball game (without competition) would be a more appropriate analogy. In a lecture transcript from the winter of 1794/95, one finds a fairly detailed description. Kant attributes here to the power of understanding the function of curbing the imagination in a certain sense. In its free play, imagination tends to become extravagant. If that happens, understanding calls it to order. Only thus is the harmonious play secured. I suggest that we take this as a somewhat misguided description of the play itself. It confuses a quite imaginable secondary component of the play with its overall constitution.

The lecture transcripts provide us with another, this time very interesting observation with regard to the play. It explains, among other things, why Kant is inclined to call also the play itself (and not only the performance of the imagination) "free" and why he could very well describe the entire state of the mind within the play as a state of freedom. Our knowledge depends upon the operations of powers that are very different in nature and origin. Hence the acquisition of knowledge inescapably depends upon mutual coercion: our understanding is *restricted* in its usage to what is given in intuition, and our imagination has to *serve* under the understanding's principles of unity. "They are like two friends who dislike but can't relinquish each other, for they live in a continuous fight and yet can't do without each other" (AA XXIV,1,p.707). Taking up Kant's illustration, we can say that only in the aesthetic situation does the fight come to an end, the coercion cease, and an unconstrained accordance prevail. It is no surprise that such a state will be experienced with pleasure.

This way of accounting for the play derives directly from what is distinctive in the foundation of Kant's epistemology. Although it is only an illustration, we are permitted to take it seriously. But then it becomes indispensable to qualify another of Kant's assertions, which is to the effect that the harmonious play is a *prerequisite* for the possibility of knowledge. It has become totally impossible to read this as amounting to the claim that only through an aesthetic situation are we capable of acquiring empirical knowledge. But another reading suggests itself immediately: the harmonious agreement of the cognitive powers arises, albeit only in comparatively rare perceptual situations, from *nothing but* the fundamental constitution of the powers in question. Consequently, we have the right to assume that it is a possible state of every mind whose knowledge is of the same kind as ours. But then we also have the right to expect that all human beings will eventually agree with our own well-considered aesthetic judgments. This suffices to justify the claim of a distinctive a priori validity that is inseparable from aesthetic judgment.

The theory of the harmonious play of imagination and understanding provides Kant with the most important resources of his critique of taste and thus of the most innovative part of the *Critique of Judgment*. His language of faculties and powers of the mind can easily strike the reader as archaic. But we have seen that it can be translated with ease into a language of cognitive operations. And that, within the present philosophical climate, sounds less obsolete than it did two decades ago. Besides, one should always assess the merit of a theory by its illumination of the facts of its intended application. We already began to realize that Kant's accomplishments in this regard are impressive. To be sure, he refrained almost altogether from specifying how his theory can be put to work in an analysis of aesthetic experience. That he himself felt that he lacked clarity about some features of the theory is in part responsible for this failure. I have tried to clarify and substantiate Kant's fundamental theorem and to produce an improved version of it, but exclusively with means Kant himself provides and also alludes to.

In conclusion, I would like to indicate a merit of a Kantian aesthetics that should win it a place among contemporary aesthetic theories. Kant is certainly a formalist. He is committed to the view that beauty and all other elementary and purely aesthetic qualities depend exclusively on the formal arrangement of a perceived manifold. He aligns himself with the tradition that conceived of aesthetic phenomena in light of the formula "Unity within the manifold." It is, however, well known that the formula is vague; it is difficult to assign it a precise meaning that does not render aesthetic analysis either counterintuitive or circular. This has frequently led to the charge that formalism in aesthetics is unpromising or outright inadequate. On the other hand, formal analyses are indispensable in evaluating aesthetic qualities and artistic achievements.

The well-known formalist theories of this century are really lacking a serviceable notion of form. Such a notion would have to distinguish mathematical and ontological form from aesthetic form. It would also have to avoid the theory of the formation of gestalts, which is too weak to explain what is distinctively aesthetic. Besides, the form of aesthetic objects exhibits tensions and contrasts that are encompassed or dissolved by a dynamics that is an essential aspect of the form as such. This observation gave rise to theories that interpret form as an expression or a projection of bodily tensions and movements. But this leads, unfortunately, to the removal of the aesthetic experience from the processes of cognition. One would have hoped that the most prominent contemporary theory, that of Nelson Goodman, would improve the situation. But to the extent that he tries to account for aesthetic form, it can be shown that Goodman's theory is caught in a circle.

A theory of the Kantian style must become attractive in such an environment. It preserves the close connection between the aesthetic experience and the fundamental structures of cognition. It also accounts for cognition in terms of mental activities. Thus it might be in a better position to come up with an analysis of the dynamics within aesthetic form.

Finally, while it is a formalist theory, it distinguishes clearly between ontological and mathematical form on the one hand and aesthetic form on the other. Even after two hundred years, it remains promising to pursue such a program. Kant himself encourages us to do so and not to confine ourselves to the words of the *Critique of Judgment*, which (I quote again) established only "clearly enough that the principle has been stated correctly" (1st ed., p. x).

II

APPLICATIONS

THREE

The Contexts of Autonomy:
Some Presuppositions
of the Comprehensibility
# of Human Rights

WHEN EVERYTHING has been done to proclaim human rights; when everything has been said to show that human rights are norms with a claim to validity and universality; when every effort has been made to show that such claims can be rationally justified on the basis of universal principles alone; when every relevant feature of their potential for cultural imperialism has been taken into account; when, in fact, there is strong evidence to show that human rights today are set in a wholly different global context than that of their original modern constitutional proclamation and theoretical justification—even after all this, it is difficult to see how human rights claims can be championed and made effective if, even tacitly, they are regarded as fictions, however beneficial and cornucopian, and not as truth. Yet this suspicion is as widespread as is the sense of impotence in which human rights discourse is almost ineluctably mired.

What can philosophy do to check the further diminution of human rights discourse? Its greatest contribution may be in helping to reinstitute belief in the truth of human rights claims, not through a revival of past historical contexts alone, as some philosophers have sought to initiate, but through an analysis of human rights themes, claims, and hopes in their historical context of interrelated convictions and prospects, along with an interpretation of subsequent changes in these contexts and the exploration of possible ways to justify norms within them.

Theoretical attempts to interpret human rights have notoriously tended to disregard the contexts in which human rights claims are anchored, and therefore to overlook entirely the far-reaching shifts from modern to contemporary thought contexts. This oversight may be due, in part, to the attempts by exponents of contemporary practical philosophy— whether variants of general-utility or general-will theories, of empiricist ethics or rationalist moral theories—to remain methodologically consistent within the broad frame of classical practical philosophy. Rigid adherence to a particular type of theory and its distinctive mode of argument, however, assumes that the truth of human rights claims can be made dependent upon the success of such a theory. But no theory is airtight; all can become subject to fundamental doubt. And if they do, so too does the validity of any human rights claim they might make. Even more, contemporary practical philosophy seems unable to articulate the inner perspective of the individual agent who has doubts and reservations about the normative conduct invoked by human rights claims.

To preserve the tradition of human rights in a transformed world, without succumbing either to superficial, nostalgic sentiment or to nagging suspicions that it is little more than a moral fiction, requires a theory that is sufficiently broad to incorporate what is often neglected and sufficiently bold to withstand the temptation for tidiness and harmony at any price. Such a prospect may enable us to *rethink* human rights, rather than to indulge in violently exaggerated reactions to the cant and vanity of earlier generations.

Preliminary Questions Regarding the Grounding of Rights

At the time of their first constitutional proclamation and justification, human rights were legal entitlements that, unlike other entitlements, developed pathos and triggered intense motivations. Both in the United States and in France, the majority of those who acknowledged and justified human rights, and who acted in accordance with them, were of the opinion that this pathos and motivation were supported with good reasons. Human rights, they believed, were based on valid, universal norms. It was inconceivable to them to explain human rights in terms of hidden interests or as a fiction for the integration of a newly emerging social system. If we are to reestablish the truth of human rights claims in a contemporary formulation, we must once again take seriously what is today widely discarded: belief in valid, universal norms.

Before taking up this formulation, it might be useful to introduce some easily ignored philosophical distinctions. To begin, norms are ideas about the proper ordering of conduct in the world. As such, they incorporate a notion of the world in which they would be realized. The use of norms cannot occur if they are not related to the factual circumstances of the world in which they are brought into play. The ideal of bravery, for example, makes as little sense in a world without danger, as does that of conservation in a world that husbands its resources.

Second, norms embody a specific notion of the agent who is governed by them. For the ideal of bravery, the notion is of an agent who can effectively confront life-threatening circumstances; for the ideal of prudence, one who can effectively govern the human tendency toward prodigality. Thus, when we adopt a norm, we do so because it has bearing for us; in knowing this, we simultaneously recognize ourselves as agents of a particular kind.

The correlation of world- and self-images in norms was first noted by Kant and those who followed him. For them, the variability of our images of ourselves and of the world we inhabit has far-reaching consequences for philosophical analysis: it means that the way an agent sees itself—its self-image—is no more readily deduced from a particular social world than it is from a purely abstract norm. To be sure, some of our self-images as agents do derive from our position within a particular social system. Moreover, social systems inform our sense of personal identity as well. Nevertheless, we are not wholly determined by our environment. The course of life can lead through numerous, differing self-images that may conflict. Because we are confronted with differences in outlook that both relate to and limit each other, we find, when we work through these conflicts, that of necessity we appeal to a more general and encompassing world understanding than that afforded by any specific natural or social worldview. It is this more general world-image, however variable, that is constitutive of the form of an agent's self-image.

How we construe both the order of the world and the place of agents in that world contributes as much as, if not more than, anything else to the self-images we have of ourselves as agents and to the interpretation of the arena within which we understand and accept norms for our conduct. To speak of rights as norms is to speak of a world in which an agent's conduct is to be regulated: some acts are required; others precluded; still others are guaranteed. But whether guaranteeing a sphere of freedom in which the agent can act, or assuring the minimal conditions under which the agent might live, the notion of rights is inseparable from the conditions of the factual world. This is not to suggest, however, that the principle of rights applied to real-world conditions is derived wholly from that world; in some sense, any normative principle differs from the factual world insofar as it is an ideal for, rather than a reflection of, the ordering of the world.

Clearly, not all correlations of world- and self-images are conducive to the adoption of rights as norms. Three correlations proceeding from different images of the world may help to illustrate this point.

One view is of the world as the *intentional object* of our actions, a world in which our actions are part of a natural life cycle or serve to maintain the natural or cosmic order. In such a worldview, we would see ourselves as agents whose actions conform to and reflect our knowledge about the fundamental processes of the natural life system. And in such a world, perseverance and acceptance of fate are the norms that would bear most strongly on our lives, for these serve to sustain the life cycle. These norms also underscore the embeddedness of the agent in the world structure. But because world-image, self-image, and norm do not allow independent reflection on the conditions that enable possible courses of conduct, a prospect that is fundamental to the establishment of entitlements is absent. And without this prospect, human rights can have no place in this world.

Another view that secures at least a measure of independence for the agent is of the world as an order already constituted, but as *only a framework* for our actions. For us to comprehend the order, we must conceive of some authority who is both the author (god) of the order and independent guardian of the world. The transcendence of this god opens the prospect of the agent's conceiving of itself as independent. It does so because the agent is a member of two spheres—the present one and another, redemptive one. In the present sphere, there is an obligatory ordering that determines the agent's place and course: the agent knows both its role in life and what is required of it. The redemptive sphere places obligations on the agent as well: the god calls upon the agent to practice brotherly love. The goal and fulfillment of life is thus grounded in the redemptive sphere. This requirement to practice brotherly love introduces another dimension to the agent's self-interpretation: the agent now conceives of itself as the origin of activity that is appropriate to the redemptive sphere and that is the vehicle through which the agent is ultimately brought "before god." By virtue of its response to the call for brotherly love, then, the agent can move beyond the present world order, thereby incorporating a measure of transcendence into its self-image. Yet the universal call to brotherly love, while transcending the boundaries of regionalism, of race, and of culture, nevertheless belongs to the redemptive sphere and not to the present one. Although this call may cause us to weigh our conduct in the present sphere differently, it does not restructure our conduct. The call to brotherly love is not a universal ethic for action in this world. Despite the independence from this world sphere that the individual gains through its transcendence to the redemptive one, no conception of human rights can emerge in this correlation: this image of the world fails to promote the sense of self-determination necessary to direct independent reflection back toward the world order of the present sphere.

But there is another way of conceiving the world, one that enables us to fill in this lacuna. We might imagine the world simply as a field that can be shaped according to norms that only we as agents can bring into play—a world that is not itself a source of norms, and still less a receptacle of norms bestowed by an authority above. The agent in this world has the self-image of being the sole source of both actions and norms. These are imposed upon the world through knowledge of laws and technical transformations, and established there in social institutions and in the constitutional state. The norms that bear upon this agent's self-image are entirely self-derived and self-referring: they have to do with individual self-preservation, not in the sense of survival in a hostile world, but in the sense of instituting a world shaped by reason alone. This worldview/self-image, together with its norms, is hospitable to the notion of human rights. For a principle that has its origin in the agent and that can serve as the foundation for the construction of a political constitution, while simultaneously orienting all conduct, even beyond the reach of any particular society, is integral to the universal scope of rights entitlements.

The three outlooks not only illustrate the structured interdependence of worldview, self-image, and norm, but also bring into view the role of motivation. What might conceivably motivate us is unintelligible apart from the self-images we hold. As self- and world-images of an agent vary, so also do the forces that encourage the adoption of certain norms. Agents who experience the world as the nexus of fate have motivations quite different from those of agents who experience the world order as providential, and more different still from those of agents who experience it as opening up spheres of emancipating action. Within the entire range of motives commensurate with the self-image we hold, it must be possible for norms to be the decisive motivating factor in our conduct. If this were not so, norms would either be regarded as objects of intellectual inquiry and historical reflection—useful devices for the interpretation of conduct, but not for its motivation—or as necessary fictions for societal regulation. To hold that norms do motivate conduct does not require the belief that all norms function in the same way. Norms can dominate an entire life, just as they can be held in check in all but special circumstances; they can be placed above question, or they can be subjected to critical scrutiny. Nevertheless, norms that are consonant with the agent's self-image and world-image are capable of constellating motives and of producing sufficient pathos to incite action.

The interrelationships of worldviews, self-images, and the acceptance of norms that motivate action are indeed complex and difficult to articulate conceptually, yet they are nonetheless integral to conceiving the vision of life that those who used the language of rights as a natural expression for it must have had. We may not understand their experiences, but these experiences cannot be excised from an interpretation of the original proclamation of human rights. To do this would deny us the possibility of discerning the inner perspective of those who first embraced rights, and would obscure the fact that the idea of rights carries a world concept with it. To omit is inevitably to restrict. The narrow view that considers human rights only as norms tacitly presupposes that a broader range of considerations, such as the conditions under which human rights norms will be adopted or the conditions under which they will become truly persuasive, at best belongs to the past if it was ever viable at all. For this reason, those who hold the narrow view cannot understand that the resistance of other cultures to the propagation of human rights programs is in reality resistance to a worldview or to norms that may be adopted as political or rhetorical expedients, but not as decisive motivations for conduct.

The Modern Grounding of Rights

At the root of eighteenth-century philosophical arguments for human rights stood an idea of the world and its relation to human society as a single intelligible structure. This idea, the philosophical arguments, and the first constitutional proclamation of rights were all received by, and resonated with, the general consciousness of the time; at least some of these arguments were based on world conceptions that could evoke pathos in those who embraced them.

These arguments followed two theoretical lines, one dominated by Locke and Paine, the other by Rousseau and Kant. Both lines of thought held two ideas in common: they ruled out the natural sphere of human activity, as such, as a source of norms, and they developed a concept of reason according to which the form of reason itself is both the only and the sufficient source of rules and obligation for action. From these lines of thought, the modern idea of an "autonomy" of reason and of the rational human essence emerged. Not only actions, but also the norms for action, were thought to issue from this self-relation, self-organization, and self-development of reason. Moreover, the basis for the legitimacy of norms was claimed to reside in reason. It followed from this that the natural world is subject to the imposition of an order that has been rationally derived through technological transformations and constitutional social organization. No longer bound to the limited task of protecting life from natural adversities, human conduct could now transform the basic drive of self-preservation into a rational form of conscious life that followed norms derived solely from reason's understanding of itself.

Autonomy thus conceived became the backdrop for a type of theory that is explicitly based upon the conditions and needs of life (Locke). From these basic needs, legal entitlements were derived that not even the power of the state could violate, even though the idea of the state flowed from the same source. Difficulties arise for this type of theory, however, as soon as "reason" is introduced to explain the universality, reciprocity, and obligatory nature of rights, since reason is not inherent in the set of needs that gave rise to theory.

Autonomy is also an element in the type of theory that departs from the self-relation of reason and proceeds to define "man" solely on the basis of autonomy (Rousseau). Here, rational self-preservation explains consciousness and the dynamically far-reaching self-shaping of human life. This dynamic renders the essence of man as nothing other than freedom, which is emancipation both from external influence and from previous impositions of norms. Accordingly, the function of rights, and the duty of government, is not to guarantee the opportunity for the self-shaping of life, but rather to promote the integrity of self-determination in human creative action.

The critical power generated by the interaction of these two types of theory was altogether extraordinary. It precipitated the collapse of social orders in which norms were attached to worldviews that no longer seemed tenable, offering instead a new understanding of both norms and freedom. A new self-consciousness and a new self-confidence in the race appeared. Insofar as the norms of the new self-consciousness were self-legitimating, its distinctive character emerged more from its establishment of new orders than in rebellion against the old. In this framework arose belief in the original rights of man; here, they found support and background.

The capacity to conceive of multiple ways of categorizing reality, like the ability to understand what it is to be an outcast, a revolutionary, or a pauper, permeated the temper of the time; it centered in Rousseau. It was clear to him that the framework within which the belief in the rights of man arose needed further elaboration. From the perspective of the agent who has become conscious of freedom, it is unsatisfactory to locate this freedom in the simple relation between individual self-determination and the meaningless material world. So Rousseau added, as the correlate of the conscious life that establishes its norms from within, a richer picture of the world, one that included the basic deistic tenet of a god who supports the goals of free self-actualization. And those who followed Rousseau broadened this view further by maintaining that the life of human freedom is reflected in the common ordering manifest in the beauties of nature.

But even this image, which Rousseau dedicated to the individual who lives under the self-image of autonomy, was soon thought to be inadequate. Its basic flaw seemed to lie in its assumption that isolated individual freedom is the Archimedean point of all worldviews. So to the Rousseau-inspired faith in freedom, Kant and his successors added an important qualification: freedom finds support and opens up possibilities for life only in a world-image of which it genuinely becomes a part; the world, in turn, must be thought to include both the potential for generating self-determined freedom and the site for the appearance of freedom.

From reflections of this order emerged attempts to transform the dominant deterministic world-image of the time (Spinoza's)—which shared many components with the theory of autonomy—in a way that opened a place for the rational self-determination of the finite being. Thus emerged the ideal of a "Spinozism of freedom," which remained influential well into the nineteenth century. Many now consider Hegel's work, which combined methodological monism and autonomous freedom, to be proof of their potential for opening a theoretical path and for penetrating the experiences of his time. Fichte, who alone attempted to make autonomous action intelligible without presupposing the notion of the person as a fixed starting point, also designed such a path. This approach made it possible to introduce questions that cannot be anchored solely in the concept of the person— questions such as those about the origins and development of the structure of consciousness—without, in the course of answering these questions, turning the belief in freedom into a fiction.

Although many today find such theories obscure, no one

can deny the value of a theory that was committed to, and brought together—however irreconcilable they appear—the premises an epoch refused to abandon. Of greater value still is the capacity of this type of theory to offer an interpretation of the autonomous agent's worldviews that does not derive its power of articulation from another worldview that is based quite differently. But perhaps the greatest value of this type of theory is that it opens the way for connecting worldviews of freedom and worldviews of other cultures within a single theoretical context. A conspicuous example of this potential may be found in the way this type of theory interprets history. History, it says, consists not only in progress toward liberation, but also in the self-development of the human spirit; and only when the human spirit is cultivated into the consciousness of freedom and self-certitude does the basic constitution of spirit, operative at each stage of its development, become manifest.

This type of theory has further potential; its analysis of human freedom could perhaps be revived. But whatever might result from such a revival, it is certain that this type of theory, just like that of Locke or Rousseau, cannot be restored by simply calling up the past. A shift in the consciousness of the age and its perception of problems makes this impossible. This shift escaped the theoretical gaze of thinkers of the early nineteenth century, yet it wholly changed the prospects for communicating and justifying human rights.

The Shifts in Contexts

It often appears as if, in our time, the universal lip service paid to human rights stands in inverse relation to subtle social and institutional communication of egoistical self-images. Our approval of human rights reflects an Enlightenment worldview of self-interest that contributed to the institution of legal recourse for the adjudication of rights disputes. Our egoistical self-images, which also reflect Enlightenment ideals, nevertheless incorporate a propensity for nihilistic practices that can erode both norms and institutions. We may justly wonder why these conflicting forces seem to correspond in our contemporary perspective.

The more deeply we look into the worldview within which the theory of autonomy operated and within which the idea of human rights made its modern appearance, the clearer it becomes that this outlook emerged from what may be called a second level of critique or a *second level of reflectedness*. This orientation of thinking goes beyond a simple account of the possibility of error in general, characteristic of a first level of critique, to incorporate the awareness that misconceptions can inform our ways of knowing and that these may well originate in the way we reason. Reflection upon the sources of knowledge is therefore recognized as indispensable to the possibility of reliable knowledge.

The emergence of critical thought that turns upon itself was fundamental to the discovery that norms can have their source in nothing other than the self-awareness of reason. Whether valid or invalid, discourses that proceed from the inward turn of reason become the basis for the insight that reason is the source of norms. Paradoxically, not only calm, rational insight, but also a peculiar *pathos* of reason, manifested as intense feelings of self-empowerment, issue from critical reflection. Even though rational discourses can in fact be the basis of error, the critical capacity of reason can be the foundation of a life free from outside control and confusion.

But the coalescing of these forces in reflective thought can precipitate a *third level of reflectedness*. Whereas the second level of reflectedness seeks sources of deception that insinuate themselves systematically into the structure of our cognitive capacities, the third level suspects that all rational suppositions are themselves nothing but irresistible deceptions. Whereas the second level of reflectedness generates the pathos of rational self-determination, the third level, in the course of confirming its suspicions, arrests this pathos.

The third level of reflectedness gained predominance in the middle of the nineteenth century. It gave rise to theories which claimed that life directed according to reason and self-determination is an illusion, and that it is the basic struggle for survival and the need for intense feeling, not autonomy or the pathos of freedom, that support this illusion. Of course, such theories served to reinforce the third level of reflectedness. However much they differed, they were nonetheless as one in unmasking and rejecting the basic convictions that had given rise to the notion of human rights.

A variant of this third level of reflectedness, developed by the new science of sociology, was used in two ways to explain the historical proclamation of human rights as a development of social forms: "human rights" was interpreted as the battle cry of the propertied bourgeoisie, but also as a basis for the dismantling of stratified society and for promoting a merely functionally differentiated form of society. In both interpretations, human rights are construed as a weapon to be used in a struggle, but one whose inexorable resolution human rights—paradoxically—cannot support. Still, merely to construe human rights as a weapon offers new means for understanding the intense fervor its proclamation evoked. By way of contrast, the rationality of the third level of reflectedness, which exposes illusions, wholly checks pathos.

Yet the sobriety of the diagnostic gaze is in some ways self-refuting. In a world stripped of its deceptions, everything real is meaningless. We view the world as an illusion, all world-images as repudiated, and world events as unalterable. Nothing remains to motivate us except the urge to seek refuge in an inner sanctuary, where warnings against the thoughtless suspension of norms are mere rhetoric and not, as they had once been, a belief in the ruling power of reason. Thus, extolling the rejection of reason's exuberance can come to entail both emotional hostility and a latent desire to restore what has been lost to illusion: the primary need for self-esteem.

To restore self-esteem, the claim that the illusion of rationality must be dispelled was coupled with the claim that humans could fulfill themselves through the imposition of spontaneous, self-created form on the chaos found in the worlds of nature and thought. By the end of the nineteenth century, the appropriate form was thought to be the *polis*. Characterized by instinctive and spontaneous cooperation, the *polis* is our own construction, an invention. Rationality may well confuse such constructions with eternal laws or divine decrees, but this is fatal delusion. Behind the veil of rationality, it was now to be argued, lies the prospect that all action can be oriented and organized in the service of an order of nature or of an actual dynamic of societal development. This apocalyptic prospect foretells the great human uprising of the children of light against the children of darkness, of the fighters for freedom against all the stifling oppression of remorselessly tidy rational organization. Herzen, Proudhon, Bakunin, Kautsky, and Sorel spoke in similarly revolutionary terms. Their doctrines of political salvation tended either to accept covertly or to flaunt a deliberate nihilism as their basic position: the crippling views of the meaninglessness of everything real are turned into violent forms of radical action, untrammeled by illusions. Such radical actions first appeared toward the end of the nineteenth century under the guise of *Realpolitik*, which divorced politics from the realm of ideals and morals. In the first part of the twentieth century, these actions had, as a further consequence, the historically unparalleled torment, degradation, and annihilation of human beings. These consequences suggest that deliberate nihilism must be interpreted as a revolt against the belief in reason as such and its derivative doctrine of human rights—a revolt staged by those who not only hold this belief to be empty, but who also fancy themselves to be serving the cause of truth.

The *horror* of the revolt and its policies of annihilation had several concrete effects: it gave strong new impetus to attempts in the early twentieth century to revive the natural-law tradition as a way to support rights; it had a far-reaching impact on UN efforts, buoyed by the revival of this tradition, to forge a new Declaration of Human Rights; and it led to the establishment within the European community of the first international institution for claiming human rights in court. Furthermore, it played a part in the recent return of philosophical ethics to the classical theoretical tradition of grounding norms rationally. Yet new variants of deliberate nihilism continue to manifest themselves in heretofore unthought ways; in numerous countries, the mass graves of many of its victims give silent testimony to this.

No doubt, the most noble motives and the most pressing causes are integral to the defense of civilization against the nihilistic practices that weaken its foundations. But motives and causes are not enough. In order to oppose nihilism effectively and perspicuously, motives and causes must be conjoined with a valid theory that can give rise to justified convictions. Because nihilism *in action* is a direct attack upon the basic convictions that underlie human rights, it is absolutely clear that for a valid theory to give rise to justified convictions, it cannot be restricted to an analysis of norms alone. Nihilistic practices, after all, know themselves to be supported by a worldview, and they perceive the norms of human rights doctrines to be empty when they are not anchored in the world; even where nihilism is overtly rejected, many of its elements can make their way into unarticulated opinions concerning the insignificance of human life and the baselessness of universal norms. The worldview of nihilistic practices offers a different type of self-image, one derived from the attempt to intensify the energies of ancient kinds of action by liberating them from the control and inhibition of illusion. But nihilistic self-images, of course, are imaginary because they are derived from motives that do not develop naturally from a world-image, but erupt with the belief in the *dissolution* of former world-images. Imaginary though they may be, nihilistic self-images are nevertheless potent because they locate the acceptance of norms, no matter how destructive, in the nexus of self-world correlations. They therefore approximate more nearly the conditions of reality than do the views that conceive rationally defined ethics so narrowly that they overlook entirely the contexts upon which the acceptance of norms depends.

Anyone who wants to conduct a critical examination of practical nihilism, exposing *its* illusory structure, must have at hand elements of a theory of corresponding depth. Taken by itself, criticism of this order would not yet consist in the justification of human rights or in the grounding of our conviction of their existence in action, but would merely restore the cool distance of the third level of reflection. If not combined with another interpretation of the world, such an examination would leave us utterly confused, with our impulse to act paralyzed, and situated in a context from which nihilistic practices could easily reemerge.

Now other forms of criticism have appeared. Both the philosophies of "concrete existence" and of "scientific socialism" see the third level of reflectedness to be continuous with its predecessors, which first made possible modern liberal individualist and general-will theories about human rights. Both philosophies aim to strike down second-level theories of rights and third-level nihilism simultaneously by showing that second-level theories of autonomy led straightway into aggressive nihilism.

To begin, the two philosophies see nihilism operating not

only in political doctrines of apocalyptic salvation, but also in the technological powers of our time. Industrial and state bureaucracies assume that the mind is itself a machine that orders and masters material reality. But if the mind is a machine, recollective and imaginative capacities atrophy. Thus, the triumph of technology is the liquidation of the individual and its values.

At a more fundamental level, these theories maintain that the true origin of our current malaise is the assumption of third-level reflectedness that man can set himself up as the measure of all order and as the source of binding world meaning. They go on to say that this assumption of egocentrism was also basic to the second level of reflectedness. Thus they claim that the enthusiasm evoked by the first proclamation of human rights actually contained in embryonic form the greatest threat to all humanity.

To rescue humanity from this threat, these philosophies maintain, we must experience our place in the totality of what is in a fundamentally different way. To do this, we must be released from all the conditions that have informed our thinking for the past two centuries. Apart from this, all we can contribute to the possible future of the race is the recognition of our own historical situation and our abstention from all egocentric claims.

Although these philosophies appeared to be in decline, they have begun to reemerge as a philosophical force. Once again we are counseled to withdraw our claim to human rights. We are also admonished to eschew self-critical examination and the technical apparatus that is thought to provide a better life. What this admonition ignores, however, is their indispensability to our lives. Even our new sensitivity to our own physical world and the universe is made possible and sustained by our third-order-of-reflectedness thinking and its offspring, technology. The call to cast aside the imprudent use of technology, as well as the entire third level of reflectedness, must—to be consistent—include the invocation of a self-image that has mythic origins. But once we recognize that the mythical world-images corresponding to mythical self-images leave little room for the view that the world is tender or friendly, and less room still for concern about the endangered living place of the race, we should hesitate. Such mythical world-images are untenable in our time. To be honest with ourselves, we must reject not only them, but also those calls to deconstruct society that are based, however tacitly, upon them.

If the third level of reflectedness is historically continuous with the rationality that led to the proclamation of human rights, we have only one alternative: we must either decide to stabilize ourselves within our predicament, holding out as our brightest prospect only cool detachment from our own existence, devoid of interpretation; or else find in the world situation grounds for self-images and an interpretation of our situation that again opens our conscious life to the acceptance of universal norms.

The interpretation of our contemporary world demands first of all that we discard the notion that man—the finite subject—is the axis around which the world turns and evolves. What Rousseau intimated, Kant and his successors saw more clearly: we can understand ourselves only as part of a world, a world that includes within it the possibility of freedom. To be sure, there are those who will claim that adopting such world-images is no more than a way of appropriating the benefits of hindsight in order to stabilize social conduct. For these claimants, images of autonomy are consciously false; nevertheless, they say, we employ such images, despite their discontinuity with the world we experience, "as if" they were true, owing to their usefulness for ordering conduct in the ordinary world. But adopting images in this way, while presumably serving the interests of society, actually serves the needs of the individual. Because such adoption has, primarily, cognitive use-value, it covertly enthrones the finite subject and its needs.

The charge of egocentrism, even tempered by the form of an "as if" philosophy, cannot, however, extend to the most powerful images of freedom. One of these is the unity in freedom of the autonomous agent and the world, even though both agent and world derive from opposing forces. Another is of the autonomous agent who confronts the sensuous embodiment of freedom in beautiful appearances, because the form of the beautiful is free-flowing. Both images underscore the experienced continuity between self and world in freedom. But these images and others like them in the history of autonomy are further bound together through the conviction that norms and knowledge of their validity are grounded in a sphere other than the ego. They proceed from an inner form of self-conscious life that extends beyond our sense of self-assurance, to become integrated into a total world-image.

We can only incorporate this conviction—that the ground of freedom differs from the self—into those comprehensive images that transcend seriously the agent's self-assertion. This means, among other things, that we must conceive of the finite subject in new ways. We can, for example, entertain the notion of a subject from whom a normative principle may be derived, even though the subject does not yet have a self-image or self-generated motivation. We need only note that such a subject need not be conceived of as an entity that explains or generates itself. Something may exhibit the form of a closed and complete system, yet be founded upon grounds that are not accessible within the system itself. To think of ourselves in this way is to recognize that because we are not wholly self-contained, we could not possibly generate the pathos of freedom. We can still legitimately orient conduct with respect to what we do know about the structure of the finite subject, but we must remember that the pathos of freedom, which issues through us, has its origin in another source.

If we organized our conduct according to such a self-image—according to which we are capable of discerning the structure of our conscious lives without thereby apprehending its ground—we could still see ourselves as the original source of rights in a sense that is indispensable for a precise concept of human rights. We could, that is, base the legitimacy of human rights claims—claims to a life attaining insight and practical understanding and to the minimum means without which such life could not be supported—solely upon the inner form of our conscious life. Moreover, on this basis, we could conceive of ourselves as having sufficient power to assert these claims for ourselves and others. In this strict sense, we would remain the *origin* of human rights entitlements.

This does not mean, however, that our entire self-consciousness depends upon these claims: it would be otiose to hold that we are ourselves only to the extent that we actually assert these claims. What protects these claims from such empty pride is a larger context, one in which the possibility of infringements is real; apart from this, "human rights" would be not only instruments for the self-enhancement of our lives, instruments that help us to ignore or overcome our experience of finitude and dependence, but also ploys for transforming the legitimacy of human rights into arrogance. Unrestrained pride, then, precipitates forms of arrogance that undermine human rights still further.

At a time when the earth is overpopulated, when we seem to be taught our own nothingness, and when belief in human rights is not steadfastly supported—at a time, in short, that is dangerous precisely because we need to believe in human rights and do not—we must, to thwart those forces that threaten to destroy us, adopt a meaning of personhood for our world that offers us a self-image free from illusion. Such a concept would have to incorporate the inseparable connections between two apparently contradictory insights: that we as persons are the origin of rights claims, and that we are—just as originally—the only place where the world makes possible a transitory consciousness in and through ourselves. To think of ourselves in this way underscores our responsibilities to think clearly and to serve the interests of freedom. This concept affirms the free process of our self-consciousness and at the same time provides a vantage point where we may be emancipated from the vanity of our unquestioning self-centrism.

Without the legitimacy of this orientation, the tradition of human rights must be deemed ungrounded and obsolete, for the concept of right in the proclamation of the original "rights of man" depends upon the idea that every human being is a source of justifiable universal principles that bring human conduct under guidance. Even if the power of this idea to convince were to dissipate, the virtues of sympathy and compassion, the contempt for exploitation and tyranny, and the knowledge of the destructive consequences of nihilistic practices would remain. But they would come from a source other than a form of life that claims the right and dignity of humans as its starting point.

Justification in the New Context

In a comprehensive justification of human rights, two powerful perspectives in contemporary thought must be taken into account: the perspective of societies whose histories include a tradition of human rights and that of societies whose cultures and histories do not. In the latter, for universal norms to be intelligible enough to be freely adopted, there must be a new justification. Richly articulated world-images and self-images cannot simply be imposed on cultures that are implicitly thought to be inferior or whose appropriation of norms and technologies incompatible with their very foundations threatens them with collapse. At the same time, we must preserve the insights derived from the third level of reflection, introducing them into a conceptual framework in which the idea of human autonomy is formulated in a new and potentially convincing way.

I have spoken thus far of the way in which the pathos of the Enlightenment converged with the nihilism of action; for our own time, we need a self-description and world-image that converge in a different way. To this end, two trains of thought may be adduced. From the first, we may derive formal grounds for a changed self-image of our conscious life; from the second, the foundation for a changed world-image. Here, I can only sketch their points of departure, leaving open the manner in which they are to be conjoined in a single theory.

The first line of thought emerged from two of the most important philosophical thinkers of our time, Heidegger and Wittgenstein. They agreed upon one thoroughly novel idea: that which cannot be articulated, the "dark" or the "withheld," is not only the limit of what can be known, but also a formation condition of the structures peculiar to the knowable itself. Applied to our conscious life, this insight prohibits many of the naturalistic reductions of consciousness that informed the rise of third-level reflection. Such application does not oblige us to ignore or repress our knowledge of the multifaceted limitation and of the dependence of conscious life. It shows that autonomy as an orientation for conduct can still be effective and legitimate in the context of these dependencies. It deprives nihilistic practices of their bases of articulation, since the unknowable cannot be shown to be illusory.

And it can see emerging in the humanity of conscious life, which is incapable of pathos in its self-description, a ground for meaning that has a bearing not only for this life, but also for all that is real.

The second line of thought derives from the revision of an outlook on the world associated with early modernity. At that time, a cosmology and analogously constructed theory of history emerged in which the fulfillment of the race was construed as the ultimate end of world development. But this is not the only way of viewing the world that is compatible with the thought of autonomy. Indeed, what we have since learned about the world no longer allows this view. To begin with, we have good reason for holding that our conscious life is isolated in the cosmos; moreover, we foresee a future in which the earth is to become uninhabitable; above all else, we are confronted with a threat we alone have created: nuclear annihilation. A conception of our world and its ultimate end must therefore be constructed *inversely* to the world-image and teleology of early modernity. First, this worldview would have to accord priority in its ontology to the accidental over the necessary. Then we could say that the peripheral position of conscious life in the cosmos corresponds to its privileged status. Second, this world-image would have to accord priority to the transitory over the permanent. Then we could say that preservation also has meaning where lasting stability cannot be achieved. Third, this worldview would then permit us to say of the entire world process that it arrives at what was earlier conceived of as its "end" when, despite the threat of annihilation, it opens up a limited space for a self-determined life.

Such ideas would also, if they are adopted seriously into self-descriptions, cut off the transformation of the third level of reflectedness to the nihilistic practices; shorn of "illusion," such ideas are nonetheless meaning*ful*. And they are so, without relying on convictions of bygone epochs, which the good, but helpless, will is inclined to call on whenever there is no apparent way for humanity to be at home in the present.

The kind of understanding that makes use of thoughts of this order is not suitable for aligning the discourse about human rights with the pathos that surrounded the constitutional founding of the modern state. But it will be able to speak about human rights without the reservations and duplicity that undermine the very meaning of this idea.

In societies that were wedded to the tradition of human rights from the beginning, such reservations, which have their origin in the absence of convincing justifications, can be imperceptible and unrecognized by the majority. For traditions are binding, despite doubts; at least they keep doubt in check. Moreover, human rights are anchored in the constitutions of these countries, and the reference to human rights becomes a means for expressing the unity of their society, their differences notwithstanding. To be sure, such unity does not impede the growth of conduct that is the result of nihilistic practices.

But when the discourse of human rights is used to address other cultures and traditions, every weakness of its justification has direct consequences. In these cultures, there is a subtle sensitivity to the expressive power of discourse. Educated and uneducated alike know how to elicit from the invocation to accept universalistic norms the conditions of such acceptance. Without the development of acceptance conditions that are clear, credible, and commensurate with other traditions, there can be only verbal overwhelming, not a free incorporation of alien traditions into the life form of autonomy. This overwhelming forsakes the conviction that discourse about human rights can attract spontaneous agreement. Thus a second and more far-reaching consequence is that discourse about human rights becomes meaningless.

Spontaneous agreement can only issue from a discourse that is rooted in the self-image of an agent in its implicit knowledge of itself and of its world. Such discourse is not compatible with cultural relativism. Thus rights cannot be recommended with the assertion that they belong in the bundle of the achievements of Western civilization. Still less, therefore, can rights be advocated because the traditions of the West require that they be. If one advocates rights generally, it must be because of their universal validity. But then it must be possible to clarify rights within the context of other cultures and traditions—which again implies that we acknowledge their incompatibility with some forms of life and self-image. Nevertheless, it would have to be shown that real possibilities for life are opened up within their context—and not just those from which the political institutions of the West arose.

To eliminate the risk of implicit colonization that often accompanies the importation of norms, therefore, only those societies whose traditions permit the adoption of human rights can be entrusted with their appropriation, development, and proliferation. Yet precisely herein resides the universalism upon which the essence of human rights depends. We know that cultural traditions vary widely; but that these traditions may eventually grow together in fundamental self-images of the race is the sustaining hope of human rights. If this were to happen, it would become possible to speak of humankind in a sense that differs from that of the natural species or that of a worldwide political and economic interdependence. Only then, and under new and unpredictable conditions, could the language of the "rights of man" recapture the resonance and fullness of meaning that possessed those who first championed rights in modernity.

The French Revolution and Classical German Philosophy: Toward a Determination of Their Relation

CLASSICAL GERMAN philosophy wanted to grasp the inner movements of the life grounded on reason as a single, unified structure, including its drives, emotions, and modes of striving and acting. The traditional forms of philosophical theory seemed to have shied away from that task. Given their disposition, they could not motivate a kind of inquiry able to generate an understanding of such a life and a conception in which it could recognize itself, which it could then adopt as a life-praxis and realize as its own. Thus classical German philosophy (in emulation of Rousseau) believed itself capable of gaining, for the first time since Plato, a method of thinking that could liberate life from the fog and illusion of an artificial world of concepts and could reconcile thinking with spontaneously self-developing human life.

That fundamental intention has much in common with the goal of the revolutionary movement. The feudal privileges and rituals abolished by the Revolution seemed to be of a comparably lifeless artificiality. Although establishing a rational state could be compared to the accomplishments of a construction engineer, it can also be understood as the liberation of the constitution-building powers that emerge from the rational and social nature of a people that are not deformed or corrupted.

Accordingly, the Revolution tried to bring human beings into an entirely new relationship with the world—through measures ranging from the reform of the calendar and the cycle of festivals to the establishment of a public religion, inspired equally by Rousseau and by ancient traditions. Artistic praxis, too, was placed in the service of the Revolution—a tendency that once again is comparable to the conviction, held by many founders of classical German philosophy, that the insights and attitudes communicated by art are intimately related to a philosophy that aims to liberate the subjectivity in thought.

Not only their contemporaries but also the founders of classical German philosophy themselves actually expressed the inner harmony of the two movements in a variety of ways. As examples, we can cite two passages from Fichte and Schelling. In 1795, Fichte entertained the hope of receiving a pension from the French Republic to complete his *Science of Knowledge*. Such an honor would have seemed to him (according to a letter whose date and addressee are not completely certain) to be justified for the following reasons:

My system is the first system of freedom. As that nation [France] releases man from his external chains, so my system releases him from the shackles of the thing in itself, from external influence, and presents him, in its first principle, as an independent being. . . . It was while writing about this Revolution that I was rewarded with the first hints and intuitions of this system. The system thus already belongs, in a way, to the nation; the question is whether the nation wants to appropriate it publicly and openly by giving me the capacity to propound it.

In his memorial essay for Immanuel Kant (1804), Schelling interpreted the relation of Kant's philosophy to the French Revolution as follows:

The claim that only the great event of the French Revolution gained him the general public regard that his philosophy alone would never have earned is nothing less than fictitious. A few of his enthusiastic adherents, not without perceiving some special work of fate, marveled at the coincidence of these two revolutions, which, in their eyes, were equally important. They did not realize that it was one and the same long-developing spirit that, in accordance with the distinctive features of the two nations and circumstances, expressed itself in one case in a real revolution and in the other in an ideal one.

The two remarks explain the correlation between the political revolution and the new beginning in philosophy in different ways. Fichte sees his thought as inspired and guided by the uprising of freedom in France. Schelling sees in the two movements manifestations of a single process that grounds both. It is inviting then to provide a summary of the formally possible ways of correlating the two events and to give one's own explanation an acceptably clear shape by reference to it.

The following four types of explanation can be distinguished from one another. Between the two movements there is either (1) a mere coincidence or (2) a direct real dependence. In the latter case, the governing influence can originate either (2a) in the political events or (2b) in the new beginning in philosophy. Even if the relationship is not to be explained by such real dependencies, there may, nonetheless, be (3) common and also real presuppositions at work that are grounded in transformations reaching much further back. In this case, corresponding to the factors distinguished in (2), it is best to distinguish again (3a) sociopolitical presuppositions from (3b) intellectual ones underlying the development of ideas, of modes of consciousness, or of life. But we need an explanation not only for the fact that two chains of events occurred, which need to be correlated, but also for a common feature of the revolutionary and the philosophical chains, namely, that they correspond (4) in the form of their development. In both cases, the events continually and rapidly overtook themselves, coming to an end, finally, in a precarious balance that no one could have anticipated at the outset. That correspondence in the form of their development can itself be understood either in terms of (4a) a real dependence of the two processes on each other or (4b) deeper-lying presuppositions shared by the two.

Those possible explanations do not obviously exclude one another altogether. In fact, only the claim of mere coincidence is incompatible with all the other types of explanation, and that explanation is the least probable, since a considerable number of real dependencies are indisputable. Thus, if a specific mode of explanation is preferred, that preference should only be understood as emphasizing particular important determinants—important, that is, in relation to the effective determining power and the evolution of the politico-cultural meaning of the whole process. I should say in advance that in my view, explanations 3a, 3b, and 4b must be given prominence in this sense.

Neither of the two types of explanation considered under (2) can reach deep enough. At best it can be said (in line with 2a) that the ideas that led to the Revolution were also inherent in classical German philosophy as essential motives. That is true in particular in view of Immanuel Kant's relationship to Rousseau, who, as Socrates had once done for Plato, provided Kant with all the essential motives of his thought. But the form of theorizing adopted by classical German philosophy cannot in turn be derived from Rousseau. In order to provide that, Kant had to develop a wholly new concept of knowledge and rationality, admittedly with meditations from Rousseau's "Creed of a Savoyard Vicar" before his eyes as both inspiration and confirmation. But in the further course of classical German philosophy beyond Kant's thought, which had been under way since the spring of 1789, Rousseau's model played no role of primary significance. Furthermore, the decisive influence on the path of the Revolution in France did not come only from Rousseau. The traditions originating with Locke and Holbach carried at least as much weight. It was Thomas Paine, the student of Locke, who became a member of the French National Assembly, and not Immanuel Kant.

Since the time of the Revolution itself, the rumor has circulated in Germany that the Parisian events were triggered and controlled by German secret societies. During the early stages of the Parisian Clubs, there were, in fact, contacts with the Illuminati, who—after their dissolution in Bavaria—had been newly reconstituted in northern and central Germany under Johann Joachim Bode's guidance. The publications from that time periodically enjoy renewed attention, which in turn contributes to the renewal of the conspiracy theory of the Paris Revolution (in accord with 2b). But such a conspiracy theory completely neglects the dynamics that had long been prepared in France: a centralized and autocratic monarchy had striven with conspicuous success to dissolve the feudal social order but was now itself entangled in a financial and administrative crisis. The craftsmen and shopkeepers of the Parisian center had been drawn into that crisis. Thus an explosive mixture, which no conspiring activity could have brought about, developed from motives in part adopted from absolutism and in part directed against it. The intellectual world of the Illuminati must, furthermore, be understood to be far removed from that of classical German philosophy. Adam Weisshuhn and Bode were themselves students of the French Enlightenment. And while Karl Leonhard Reinhold belonged to the Illuminati, but occupied a somewhat marginal position in their intellectual world with his philosophy, Fichte, who could really consider himself close to Jacobin inspirations, avoided participating in the political activities of the secret societies and relied on public enlightenment and spiritual transformation.

One is thus led to look further back for an explanation of the parallels between the two chains of events. The social changes in France and the heightened state of tension resulting from them have already been described above. It must now be pointed out in addition that this state of tension is to be sharply distinguished from a conflict between the feudal order and the nascent industrialized mode of production. The early capitalistic property-owning bourgeoisie did not even play a marginal role in the genesis of the Revolution. Further, it has been shown that the development of a capitalistic mode of organizing production was evidently slowed down by the Revolution. The Revolution was overwhelmingly a political, not an economic, upheaval—however it is to be explained out of the constellation of a disappearing feudal order, a central state in crisis, and the threatened petite bourgeoisie of metropolitan Paris.

At the same time, it follows from everything said so far that the explanation that appeals to model 3a is equally unable to make the emergence of classical German philosophy immediately intelligible. For the factors that together precipitated the outbreak of the revolution in France were all much less developed in the divided and economically undeveloped Germany. We must therefore grant an independent significance to intellectual processes within the totality of preconditions out of which the Revolution and classical German philosophy emerged. We must supplement model 3a with model 3b.

Max Weber is among those who have explained why a fundamental reorganization of an economic system is not possible without a prior change in the mode of consciousness and in the conduct of life depending on it. Exactly that change is also presupposed when fundamentally new forms of political organization are not just devised but carried out and permanently established. The conditions of the possibility of such changes are grounded in the human constitution and cannot therefore be derived adequately from sociohistorical development. But that they are set free in particular constellations is nonetheless a consequence of a complex path of development within which actual living conditions play a determining role.

Such transformations in the mode of consciousness organized themselves around changes in man's description of himself as an acting subject and around his understanding of the use of reason. The revolutionary political process in France and the history of the development of classical German philosophy can now be traced back in a congruent manner to a change in the self-description of human beings. The grounding for political constitution is no longer sought in an orientation toward a cosmically ordained world order or in the will of a creator or even in a natural law that, without attending primarily to the constitution of a self-determining will, prescribes the fundamental features of state organization. The organization of the state is seen, rather, as a consequence of willing subjects who are associated with one another and are constituted as a unity. To this fundamental political idea corresponds the rational concept of autonomy (which takes precedence in the theory)—the idea, that is, of a rationality that, without a fundamental orientation toward the contents of the world or toward eternally fixed, given rules, spontaneously generates ways of organizing thought and the dynamics of rational life. This, in outline, is the concept of reason of classical German philosophy.

Changes in the mode of consciousness thus lie at the foundation of both the revolutionary process and the genesis of classical German philosophy. Admittedly, we have not yet fully explained the fact that such changes issue in a theory and that they bring about a theoretical movement of very high level. In order to explain this we must now appeal to particularities of the cultural and social situation in Germany. In comparison to France, Germany in the second half of the eighteenth century had at its disposal a much more developed educational system. By the end of the Reformation, the book trade and book production had attained a very sophisticated level. At the same time, polycentrism held sway in Germany, not least in its educational system. This polycentrism must be sharply distinguished from the federalism of by and large artificially formed states characteristic of the United States and of the contemporary Federal Republic of Germany. In that earlier system there existed significant but not completely dominant centers, namely, the capital cities of Austria and Prussia. There were also smaller states in which diverse conditions and ambitions could be productively realized. At the time of the Revolution this was true to an unusual extent in Karl August's Saxony-Weimar-Eisenach, in Dalberg's Erfurt, and in the bishopric of Bamberg under Franz Ludwig von Erthal, the admirer of the reforms of Joseph II. But even by itself and without the support of these other favorable factors, polycentrism prevented the domination of the country's civilization by the society of a single capital city or court.

Language and mentality were at once thereby protected from ritualizations, and only in this way were they ready for the emergence of a form of thinking that corresponded to a changed consciousness. At the same time the literature of the country was flourishing. It set the expressive power of the German language free by relating itself back to the beginnings of the Reformation. That language had not been acknowledged for a long time as a scholarly idiom, with the consequence that it had remained free of fixed patterns of concept formation. Only now did a genuine "High German"

develop—but in a period in which the change of consciousness had generated a sensitivity to new forms of expression
rooted in life itself. Even more than other European developments (the Italian Renaissance, for example), the German lit-
erary movement was thus imbued with philosophical themes
and ideas.

With Kant, Lessing, Herder, and Jacobi, the High German
language and a new system of philosophical concepts came
into existence in almost a single course of development. The
content of these ideas had been long prepared by the Protes-
tant culture of the spontaneity of the inner life and of the reflective acknowledgment of this spontaneity. Corresponding
to this preparation in turn was the decisive significance that
the deepening of the religious experience (instead of a mere
criticism of the traditional ecclesiastical system) had for the
whole process.

That process was self-centered. Whereas around the
middle of the century the civil and intellectual achievements
of England and France had set styles throughout the Conti-
nent, starting about 1770 a separate European center of grav-
ity formed in the civilization pervading the system of German
states, specifically those of northern and western Germany.
Only toward the end of the century did it also attract attention in England and France. Thus in a world still completely
dominated by Europe, there arose—for the first time since
the German Renaissance and Reformation died in the European wars of religion—an intellectual culture shaped by
problems and themes from the German tradition.

Hence, as Schelling recognized, the distinctive conditions
in the German sphere of life are what caused the all-European
transformation of consciousness to open a space precisely
here for a theoretical creativity that was neither in degree nor
in scope inferior to the innovation of the French Revolution.
This self-centeredness explains also why the development of

classical German philosophy kept essentially in step with the process of the French Revolution without being at all externally derived (e.g., by a forced imitation) from that process. The foundational task undertaken by the Revolution in the political realm corresponded in scope and approach to the intellectual task pursued by classical German philosophy. The beginnings of both movements were marked by a breakthrough to a fundamentally new system of problems. Each was thus faced with the task of making the new problematic accessible as a whole, working it through, and achieving a durable solution. In each case, development then followed a self-sustaining and intensifying course through turns that were unforeseeable and that generated ever new problematics—so that ultimately the development did justice to its impetus, not through the actual end point, but through the total movement. That development was realized in an ensemble of attempts and achievements whose fruitfulness for both political and theoretical conceptions of order and understanding has not been exhausted even today. This doubly self-sustaining sequence, which arose out of analogous—indeed unified—sources, made it inevitable that the similarities between the two processes would become conspicuous even at the time. But all attempts to reach a consensus as to the character and sources of those similarities failed.

From the understanding we have now gained we must once more look back at the question of the ground of the whole process. What exactly makes it clear for us that the political process of the Revolution, considered as a world-historical event, could not self-sufficiently take its course on its own? What is the ultimate ground for the fact that this process found its counterpart in a philosophical movement and that it had to find such a counterpart in order to become an event of world-historical significance?

We can answer those questions by reference to insights of

classical German philosophy itself to which we have to some extent already appealed. No practice of conscious life can become stable without an appropriate self-description of this life, and an image of the world that accommodates this self-description, whether that manifests itself in theoretical form or is accessible only to posterity through the historian's analysis of informal records of self-understanding. This general principle is, however, particularly true of a political practice that is in turn based on an abstract principle or, as Hegel said, is turned upside down by being based on an idea. The principle of autonomy, the formative power of freedom, was such an idea. Precisely in such an epoch, self-understanding could not stop before attaining a fully developed theory.

It is exactly the modern idea of freedom that needs by itself and from itself to be placed in a context of an explicitly articulated conceptual system. One must achieve a description of the world within which the primary abstract, nonintuitive evidence could justifiably occupy a central position—a description of the world in which the project of a life conducted in freedom must be able to acquire legitimacy and a well-founded, coherent dynamic. Classical German philosophy, in fact, developed and opened such a context for the notion of freedom. This was not effected through an octroi or through a concern simply for the appropriate means of justification. Rather it was brought about through an intellectual effort that came entirely out of an identification with the spontaneously developing activity of reason and that gained its own orientation from this.

If the notion of freedom were not placed in such a context, it would soon be suspected of being an extravagant and blind illusion or a fiction guided by interest. Already at an early stage the revolutionary process itself and its fundamental idea were, in fact, suspected of this. Edmund Burke formulated this suspicion in the most effective way. For this reason, and because the old regime made use of this suspicion in articulating its objections to the Revolution, the development of classical German philosophy was observed with more than casual interest in England and France. Only in this way did it become the truly universal philosophy of its epoch.

Today we know of the difficulties of attempting to give the ideas of political freedom and human rights an adequate context securely grounded in contemporary consciousness. Against a background of mere verbal agreement, skepticism, cynicism, and new ways of exploitation have established themselves in many parts of the world. But the ideas of 1789 have not thereby become ineffective. Whenever stagnation and corruption spread, peoples in their liberation movements again and again call and rely upon those ideas. Thus, the same situation from which both the French Revolution and classical German philosophy in Europe emerged develops anew on the path from the originally European revolution to the global society, and it still demands the same effort aiming at an ordering of life and simultaneously at a corresponding understanding of its foundations.

With this we can also see the error of those who thought that a further and now world-historical revolution could be built upon the achievements of the completed "bourgeois" revolution, to lead mankind to an even higher stage in the realization of its freedom. They did correctly observe that the institution of political freedom is as yet not identical with the establishment of a life-context rooted in freedom. But even the revolution in France, already in the constitution of 1791, was sensitive to the problem of economic protection for the rights of freedom. Had Louis XVI decided to favor that constitution seriously, it could later have taken on social democratic features. In the proposed constitution of 1793 such welfare-state characteristics did indeed play a prominent role. But the attempt within little more than one century both to surpass and to complete the political revolution in France by a social revolution contains a simple and even easily noticeable error in thinking. The process that erupted in 1789 is in truth much more deeply rooted and aims at a wide-open and as yet uncompleted future. It determines an epoch to such an extent that it becomes impossible to burden it with a further, similar dynamic, one that guarantees the realization of freedom. The history of freedom only began in 1789, and a secure total structure for it is only gradually and uncertainly becoming visible. Those who thought that the organization of political freedom was already completed in those days, and that now it should be succeeded by a higher and more universal state of freedom, produced in our century, out of thoughtlessness and enthusiasm, putatively supported by a philosophy of history, a condition in which they pushed the history of freedom into one of its greatest crises. Certainly this was not their intention, but it happened in the face of better knowledge that was in fact readily available.

Thus we have to conclude that not only is the enterprise of 1789 unforgettable and irreversible; it is at the same time incomplete, and from the perspective of a history of mankind, its completion has not yet been secured. That enterprise is thus still the task of contemporary humanity and its perspicacity—albeit under new conditions, in particular those relating to an economically secured social justice.

This task must proceed in the by now familiar two ways: as a developmental process of the politics of a world society and as a process of fundamental understanding, which one must as such call philosophical—not in the sense of a scholarly profession that concerns itself with principles, but rather in the sense in which Kant (in agreement with Rousseau) saw philosophy as a matter for mankind as such—an issue that arises within man himself, to which he responds, and on which he depends.

In France itself a skeptical reorientation toward the political process of the Revolution is under way now, in the year of the anniversary of the Revolution. People are asking whether the Revolution was worth the sacrifices that were made for it. They speculate that those sacrifices actually delayed the economic and political development of the country by half a century. It is certainly commendable for the intellectuals of a country to oppose the tendencies to thoughtless elation in an anniversary celebration. But it is clear that an evaluation that only considers positive or negative aspects of the Revolution for the development of France alone can by no means suffice. Of classical German philosophy it can equally be said that for some time it worked to some extent against concrete political changes in Germany. To take only one example, it deprived the German Jacobins of the possibility of presenting themselves any further as an avant-garde in the thinking they had derived from France. The political programs that were developed out of the new fundamental theories of classical German philosophy, with the important exception of Kant's, in fact could be employed and exploited by the political powers that tried to stem the revolutionary process more than they helped the liberation movements that continued to insist on civil rights. But neither is this adducing of regrettable short-term political consequences a decisive argument against ascribing world-historical significance to the thought impulses of classical German philosophy. Their potential is no more depleted or completed than that of the revolutionary process in France. The aim we must strive for, freedom under conditions of peace in a complex global society, still requires a context of ideas capable of a worldwide reach. Those ideas can only be made accessible within the consciousness of the undertakings and theoretical projects that classical German philosophy developed. A thinking that took its departure and orientation from the freedom of a spontaneously developing life of reason thus converges with the organization and maintenance of political freedom within modern states and modern conditions of production, to form a single task whose nature, difficulty, and weight have not become a thing of the past for us. To the contrary, these things are even more distinct and palpable for us today than they were for the initiators and contemporaries of the epoch of the French Revolution, for we have to be prepared for misguided developments that they could not foresee. Moreover, we have to attend to the restructuring of consciousness in the matured modern world as well as to new forms of philosophical inquiry that lay as yet beyond their horizon.

Thus our reflections can finally provide the grounds for the belief that Georg Forster, politically long disenchanted, articulated shortly before he died in Paris in 1793: "I still believe in the importance of this revolution for the grand circle of human fate. I believe not only that it had to happen but also that it will give minds and capacities a new development and the path of ideas a new direction."

Library of Congress Cataloging-in-Publication Data

Henrich, Dieter, 1927–
      Aesthetic judgment and the moral image of the world : studies in
Kant / Dieter Henrich.
      p.   cm. — (Stanford series in philosophy. Studies in Kant
and German idealism)
      Includes bibliographical references.
      ISBN 0-8047-2054-1 (cl.) : ISBN 0-8047-2367-2 (pb.)
      1. Kant, Immanuel, 1724–1804. Kritik der Urteilskraft.
   2. Judgment (Aesthetics). 3. Aesthetics. 4. Human rights.
   5. Ethics. 6. France—History—Revolution, 1789–1799.
   7. Philosophy, German. I. Title. II. Series.
B2784.H46   1992
190—dc20
      CIP
92–10124

⊗This book is printed on acid-free paper.